— Praise for *Angel Whispers* —

"This is a book about revelation—and Revelation. Writing in a simple, direct style, the authors first provide a glimpse of Maudy's childhood, which explains both the history of her mystic gift as well as her derivation of the seven spiritual laws that she espouses for optimal living. This is only a preview, though, as the bulk of the book fleshes out the spiritual laws through real-life accounts of persons lucky enough to cross Maudy's path. With compassion, hope and humor, Maudy and Gail lift us up and challenge us to share the fruits of their heavenly work from earth."

—Keith Noland, Ph.D. Clinical psychologist

"After reading *Angel Whispers,* I felt truly inspired. With this book, I have gained so much spiritual insight. It gave me a better understanding of life and I know when people pick this book up, they will feel the same way."

—Jane H. Hamilton, Book Reviewer

Christina —
the Best is yet
To come
Blessings —
Gail

ANGEL
WHISPERS

God Bless
With love,
Mandy   Angels award
you!

Blessings —
Gail

© Gail Hunt

About the Authors

Maudy and Gail have coauthored multiple books (including *A Voice for Him* and *Mystic Messenger*) in the United States and Europe and given presentations based upon these books.

To Write to the Authors

If you wish to contact the authors or would like more information about this book, please write to the authors in care of Llewellyn Worldwide, and we will forward your request. Both the authors and publisher appreciate hearing from you and learning of your enjoyment of this book and how it has helped you. Llewellyn Worldwide cannot guarantee that every letter written to the author can be answered, but all will be forwarded. Please write to:

Maudy Fowler and Gail Hunt
⁒ Llewellyn Worldwide
2143 Wooddale Drive
Woodbury, MN 55125-2989

Please enclose a self-addressed stamped envelope for reply,
or $1.00 to cover costs. If outside the USA, enclose
an international postal reply coupon.

Messages of Hope and Healing
From Loved Ones

ANGEL
WHISPERS

MAUDY FOWLER
AND GAIL HUNT

Llewellyn Publications
Woodbury, Minnesota

FIRST EDITION
First Printing, 2013

Book design by Bob Gaul
Cover art: Background © iStockphoto.com/David Schrader
        Blue feather © iStockphoto.com/Guenther Dr. Hollaender
        White feather © iStockphoto.com/Tolga TEZCAN
Cover design by Lisa Novak
Editing by Ed Day

Llewellyn Publications is a registered trademark of Llewellyn Worldwide Ltd.

Library of Congress Cataloging-in-Publication Data
Fowler, Maudy
  Messages of hope and healing from loved ones: angel whispers/Maudy Fowler and Gail Hunt.—1st ed.
      p. cm.
  Includes bibliographical references and index.
  ISBN 978-0-7387-2783-7 (alk. paper)
1. Spirit writings. 2. Conduct of life—Miscellanea. I. Hunt, Gail,
II. Title.
  BF1290.F69 2013
  133.9'1—dc23
                              2012034417

Llewellyn Publications
A Division of Llewellyn Worldwide Ltd.
2143 Wooddale Drive
Woodbury, MN 55125-2989
www.llewellyn.com

Printed in the United States of America

CONTENTS

Our thanks to Llewellyn Publications for making this book possible and to everyone in the company who worked on this project—we appreciate you all! We thank our families for their support, which allowed us to continue our work so we can continue to touch hearts and reach lives. Thanks to all of you for allowing us to give you a little glimpse of Heaven here on earth. God bless.
—Maudy Fowler and Gail Hunt

INTRODUCTION

"Who am I and why am I here?" I am sure that you have asked this question of yourself at some point in your life. To understand and know your true self is a continual learning process.

Your life has been a journey. We all have experienced life's roller coaster of ups and downs. We have all had experiences, and though sometimes we don't get the desired outcome, we need to look at what has happened in order for us to learn.

I consider myself a mystic and convey messages that are delivered through angel whispers from loved ones who have passed on. People often call me the "angel whisperer." I am not a psychic or a medium. I am here to pass on messages as well as present people with positive choices. I do this through teaching self-realization and self-empowerment so that you can make personal, positive, common-sense life choices that can work with and for you.

In order to make your life light in these troubled times, we will give you the tools to find out who you are and your life's purpose and mission. You can lessen your burden with some very healing words: "I can and I will." You can continue to help yourself by positive thinking, a positive attitude, and surrounding yourself with positive people. By sharing my life experiences, I will illustrate how endurance with a positive attitude, prayer, and following seven simple elements of the spiritual law got me through to be here today.

I conduct seminars in Europe and the United States, where I pass along my wisdom and encouragement. I have observed that people genuinely want to change. Of course, there are those who resist change and simply choose not to go forward, but generally speaking, I always believe there is hope. I firmly believe that with positive thinking, people can indeed achieve positive results, and this comes from looking at various aspects of our lives through new eyes and self-realization that is being presented to you in this book.

My Ancestry

I was born and raised in the Netherlands, however, I am not your stereotypical blond-haired, blue-eyed Dutch person. My mother, Susan, was born in Sumatra, and my father, Anthony, was born in Cheribon, part of the islands of New Guinea, which was under Dutch rule.

My dear mother, Susan, was granted the gifts of prophecy and healing. She was able to communicate with spirits to foresee the future. Her innate knowledge allowed her to know exactly what to do in a medical emergency, which was evident when she assisted as a midwife at age nine.

My mother was a great comfort to our family and friends. My family home was much like being at Grand Central Station because people were always visiting to ask her for advice, wisdom, and healing. Growing up in this environment was interesting. I served tea and cookies but was not allowed to sit in on the conversations, although I was very interested in the people who visited.

My father joined the Army when he was seventeen and eventually became a sergeant for the Dutch Intelligence. During World War II, my father was captured by the Japanese and worked on the Burma Trail for five years as a prisoner of war. When he returned home, there was a lot of unrest where my parents had lived, so they relocated to the Netherlands.

When I was a child, my father told me many horror stories from his time as a prisoner of war. Even though he would have preferred to forget, it was his history and a chapter of his life that makes me feel very proud to be his daughter. He was a true hero to me.

I was always very interested in how my parents battled through so many hardships. As a result, I learned how to look at life in a more positive way: to look at my strength, never my weakness.

Discovering My Gifts

I suspected I was different at a young age. I had thought everyone heard the same things I did, and was shocked to find out they didn't. When I was eight, I had a vivid dream in which I opened up my bedroom window and saw Our Lady with her arms outstretched, looking up toward heaven, with her feet upon a globe of the Earth. I had never seen a picture of this and wondered what she was doing in Holland and outside of my bedroom window. When I told my mother about my dream, she remained very calm and simply said, "Oh, isn't that nice." She knew I had a gift, but she let me explore it on my own.

When I was eleven, I had an experience that made me and my mother realize exactly what my gift entailed. I was in my bedroom combing my hair when I looked into my mirror and saw someone in a traditional Chinese dress. I didn't know this person. She was very small and had her hands folded together and was bowing. She was floating in midair. Once I realized that she must be a spirit, I immediately fainted.

When I woke up, my mother asked, "Who did you see?" I kept telling her I didn't see anyone, but she knew better. She brought out a very old photo album—one I had never seen before—and asked me if I saw this woman. I looked at the photo and acknowledged yes. The woman, whose photo I had never seen before, was my great-grand-mother from Hong Kong.

My mother knew how upset I was upon seeing a spirit, so she told me, "Maudy, if you don't want to see, simply ask heaven to allow you to hear. The angels will assist you along your life path. It is a special gift, and you can help people."

Describing My Angel Whispers

I have the gift of prophecy, which simply means that when someone is placed directly in front of me, I am allowed to know that particular person's past, present, and future. I am only allowed to reveal what is necessary for this person to go forward in his or her life with a peaceful heart.

The best way I can describe my gift is that I hear "angel whispers" in colors, sounds, scents, and vibrations. Angels deliver messages to me from those that have passed. I actually hear a voice within my inner being, which is referred to as an interior locution. This is why I can distinguish different accents and mannerisms of speech, including different languages.

What the angels also place in front of me are different life scenarios that are played within my mind's eye, and I can visually see a life scenario that the loved one wants me to convey to someone on earth. I don't actually see the loved one who has passed or the person delivering the message through the angel on assignment, but it's like watching a scene of a movie. I only listen. I do not speak to the loved ones because the angels are the connectors. Scent is another thing that I have, whereby I can distinguish scents of different things here on earth, that the loved one wants me to relay.

With my angel whispers, I also use what I call "coat hangers" (or, as my coauthor Gail calls them, Maudisms, which are listed at the end of each chapter). This works well with everyone. For example, if I advise a person to "look up and build up," it becomes very clear to them what they need to do from now on. People have actually told me that in whatever situation they are facing—no matter how difficult—that "my voice resonates within their being," and they recite the coat hanger over and over and they feel protected and reassured that they can go forward.

This gift has caused many interesting and difficult life situations for me. I learned very quickly that people are always willing to persecute someone who is different and gifted. But through the strength my parents exhibited, I knew that I would endure as well.

My First Childhood
Memory of Angel Whispers

When I was about nine years old, a close family friend came to visit. When it came time for him to leave, I wanted to say goodbye and also had an angel message for him. Since I was very small, he picked me up so we could look each other in the eye.

With great enthusiasm I said, "Mr. Thomas, I know where your son is. His name is Paul and he has a different mommy." Everyone suddenly became quiet. I saw the look of astonishment on his face, and he gently placed me back down on my feet. I continued to say, "I know where he lives," but my mother whisked me away into the house.

I was grounded for two weeks.

This man thought that our family had betrayed a secret of his and had gone behind his back to research his past. This was not true; it was my own angelic insight that brought the information to this man. He had a child out of wedlock with a woman during World War II, lost contact with her, and believed the child was placed for adoption. However, he had no clue where the child or the mother was located.

My angel whispers instructed me to give this message in order to relieve Mr. Thomas' heartache. Of course, I didn't know that I was going to have the heartache of being punished for two weeks. It was my first harsh lesson, but it reinforced the guideline of only relaying information when it is requested.

Later in life, I was informed that Mr. Thomas found and met his child. His life and that of his child was a life situation that was solved, and everyone was able to heal their wounds and be at peace.

Sharing My Gift

For years I helped individuals by passing along messages, but I wanted to do more. I wanted to share my wisdom and knowledge with others, so I asked for assistance, and it came in the form of Gail Hunt.

We attended the same church, and I first saw Gail talking to a group of people during a meeting. When I saw her, I instinctively knew her role in my life. I told my daughter that I needed to speak to Gail. My daughter asked, "Is Ms. Gail in trouble?" I said, "No, I would like her to work with me." It was at that point that I heard Gail's mother say, "She will be good for the job."

Gail was the director of faith formation at church, so I set up a meeting with her in order to register my daughter for a class. Once I arrived in Gail's office, I noticed a photo on the desk and picked it up. It was a picture of her mother, Rita, who delivered the message to me earlier.

I passed along angel whispers from her mother during this meeting to help Gail move on. She was still carrying a lot of sadness about her mother's passing. I do not usually give messages until asked. However, I was on a mission to see if Gail would accept this journey alongside me.

It wasn't an easy mission. Gail tested me for eighteen months, trying to see if I was for real or not. She decided to accept, and I am forever grateful.

When I wanted to share my gift with more than one person at a time, Gail started to organize group presentations where we would share my general knowledge and thoughts, and then talk to people on a one-on-one basis. I call these personal encounters because I am mystic. I'm not a psychic and can't give you a reading. I encounter you, and that's when I receive the angel whispers. At this time, I am able to help the individual understand their life choices, their life mission, and their personal story.

Usually there is a lot of emotion during the personal encounters. When a person is speaking to me, I tap into their life information through the vibration of their voice, their handshake, or embrace. This is how I get to know your loved ones in heaven. The messages I deliver are information from your loved ones via angels. Some of the information is very personal and particular to the loved one who is in heaven or who I am speaking to, which can be very overwhelming and hard to comprehend.

Sometimes I ask people to spell a name in order to receive some kind of personal data necessary to assist the person in front of me. I compare it to downloading a file and watching the progress bar go from left to right. This is when I am loading my info. When I'm relaying the information, I'm trying to talk and listen to the messages I'm receiving at the same time. I often just need to stop and focus on what information I'm receiving, which can make who I'm talking to feel a bit nervous. I feel the need to explain as much as I can to the person to comfort them.

During the personal encounter, it is important to go back in time to let the person recognize where and when depression started. I refer to this particular conversation as "angel's gossip" because the loved ones in heaven will bring a situation from the past to my attention. This conversation will actually help the person in front of me let go of certain hardships or heavy baggage they have carried with them throughout their lifetime. I often say, "To know where you're going is to know where you've been."

What People Can Learn from My Gift

We often make life difficult for ourselves through our personal life choices. It is my position to help you understand life's cause and effect through a simple explanation, provided by your loved ones. This way, you will recognize that with better choices, you will have a better life.

I assist and provide information through a heavenly background check by which I will give people—and help them keep—clarity of mind. Your personal database is placed in front of me, and your pages of life are flipped like an open book right before my eyes in less than a second.

It's a very cool thing for me, but most of all, it's especially helpful for you!

When this information is shared, people are always able to recognize, acknowledge, and confirm situations and experiences directly from their own personal life journey. The information is shared to help you to face it and embrace it. You will reflect back on your life and recognize where the love, honor, and respect was replaced by stress, frustration, and depression.

Your emotional awareness will be challenged by our information. Sometimes this is difficult and painful as you may have blocked out information from your life. I refer to this as a blackout, and it can be abuse or a trauma you wanted to forget. This particular situation will keep you from living life. The repressed information actually will keep you prisoner and will block you from going forward. Since negative escalation has already taken place, you have experienced the familiar blame and guilt that controlled your life.

My role is to unblock you to let you embrace this painful part of life. I explain that in life, there is never any blame or guilt—only life experience. Blame and guilt is only for a court of law. In understanding ourselves, we have our conscience to face. The intangible gifts of love, forgiveness, and courage will help you restructure this part of your life. Of course, these choices require that you use your willpower and self-love.

Bridging Spirituality

While I retrieve information, the angels or loved ones will sometimes bring scripture to my attention. I am and was raised a Catholic, however, as a young girl, I attended a Protestant school where a local priest taught religious instruction. I often was in trouble because I had more fun listening to the angels directly rather than learning my scripture lessons. I also would correct the priest or minister when they were teaching a lesson. I had to jump in where the story was not being told correctly.

Throughout the years, Gail and I have conducted presentations in Europe and in the United States. Prior to our meeting, Gail had a position that allowed her to talk with people of many faiths and backgrounds in various churches and synagogues. This allowed our travels to expand and include these groups. Everything that Gail and I have done is by invitation—no advertising. Regardless of your religion, you can read this book and gain a spiritual knowledge of yourself. I am blessed to have Gail next to me. She was the director of faith formation in Charlotte, North Carolina, and prior to that was the director of telecommunications for the Diocese of Charlotte, North Carolina. Because Gail works on a broad faith level, she is able to bridge basic spirituality to the supernatural and tie it back to scripture that may come through the angel whispers. Her expansive journeys have helped our presentations apply to anyone.

Cryptic Messages

The messages I pass along to people may not be the easiest to understand because they are direct and exactly what I hear. But while they can be rather cryptic, they are always on target. I have people focus on the simplicity and common sense of what is being said to interpret the message. The essence of the message is to help you get through the difficult parts of your life, but sometimes it's a bit harder to understand what is being said.

A good example of interpreting cryptic messages is a conversation I had with Betty. She came to a presentation in a private home in Charlotte. She was not only curious, but very interested in my world. This normally doesn't happen at presentations. People are usually just interested in themselves and I often hear, "Maudy, what have you got for me?"

One of Betty's questions was "Maudy, do you hear people from heaven all the time?" I told her I am able to turn the long-distance frequency off by changing my own focus. With this concentration, I can focus on what I need to and only pass along information when someone asks.

During her personal encounter, Betty asked if her mom, who had passed in 1997, was well. I always think about that question, because it is a good one that I hear often. But the answer is always the same—when you are in heaven, you are well. Her mother, Renee, passed along the message that she was proud of her. Then Renee showed me a Bible and said

"Romans 9:11." Betty immediately started to cry. The previous year, Betty had joined a church, and her children needed to memorize this particular passage in the Bible, so she knew exactly what it meant.

After the tears, we laughed at some other messages Renee delivered. She kept mentioning the word "burgundy" and Betty immediately understood the message. She said, "Mom and I used to go shopping every week in her old burgundy car." A word or phrase will come through that may seem very cryptic, but the person who is receiving the message will understand. "Burgundy" was Betty's confirmation of great things to remember from the past, that her mom was just fine, and she was able to go forward on her journey.

I always find it a little comical how the messages, no matter how cryptic, come through at just the appropriate moment to get the individual in front of me to confirm what they needed to learn in order to get their life back on track. This helps them to go forward in life, and it can't get any better than that!

The Seven Elements

When I was young, I started a list of intangible gifts that I could use to get through life: love, honor, respect, patience, courage, forgiveness, and belief. I acquired these gifts from listening to stories of hardship from my parents, close relatives, and friends. I would listen to their stories and determine what got them through their troubled times. I was fascinated with what I was learning because it would help me deliver angel whispers to others. I would often choose to be with the adults and leave play time with friends for another time. I knew that if I lived these gifts and could help myself, I would be able to be the peacemaker that I was sent to earth to be and help others.

Everyone is born with supernatural gifts, but it is up to you to retain the gifts that you are given. You can rediscover these gifts by learning who you are and understanding and recognizing your own strength through life's obstacles and challenges. In order to make your life peaceful, you must live these simple elements within your own life. They may be difficult to attain at times, but once you discover the wonderful impact upon your life by living one element at a time, you will see miracles.

The path we choose in life doesn't always work out for the best, and that's when love, honor, and respect are replaced with stress, frustration, and depression. This can be because someone took our love, honor, or respect away from us. When we are unable to handle sadness, depression starts to control us. Other unfortunate situations can take place and then we lose ourselves in negative energy either consciously or subconsciously.

Through my own life experiences, I know that when emotions such as sadness or anger come into play, they affect me physically as well as mentally. Negative emotions can block or decrease your supernatural gifts. If you are able to overcome your fears and challenges, you'll be able to receive clarity in wisdom and experience so that you can deal with your own hardships and help others with theirs.

I will share stories with you where I have passed along angel whispers that have caused people to achieve one or more of the seven elements. I hope that by reading accounts about people who have achieved peace and understanding, you will be able to examine your own life and achieve your own peace and understanding.

ONE

Love

We are sent to earth for love, with love, and by love. When life throws us a curveball, we have a tendency to turn to stress, frustration, and sometimes depression. This can take our love away from us, and if we let it, then we actually become prisoners of ourselves. Love is to love yourself first, and then the world. In the following stories, you will see how people have changed their lives by embracing, and living with, love.

Rise Above with Love

Annika, a thirty-four-year-old skin therapist from Atlanta, called me for advice while she was visiting her family in Minsk, Russia. In broken English, she told me that she was very depressed and didn't know why. Her soft-spoken, sad voice revealed much more to me. She was crying as she was talking to me, and it was hard for me to understand what she was saying. I immediately prayed and asked if heaven could fill me in. Through angel whispers, I learned Annika's father had passed away when she was twelve. He explained her journey to me and said Annika had been abused when she was young and had blocked it out of her life and memory.

Life is cause and effect, so I knew had to go to the heart of the problem. The abuse was the cause of her depression. I told Annika that she had lost the love for herself. She interrupted me and said she never received love from her family, so why should she love herself?

I sensed that she was being defensive. I found it necessary to get a little stern with her, which I refer to as calling the person to the order. She got the message and was ready to listen. I explained that heaven is love and that she rejected heaven by rejecting love for herself. This is how she became a prisoner of her own life.

I knew she was in a self-destructive mode and was having suicidal thoughts, and I informed her that she was a walking time bomb. Annika silently acknowledged this as she was sobbing and crying. She told me she was unable to have a baby because of the abuse.

As I was listening to her father, he revealed more of Annika's past journey and what she was going through. I brought the element of love to her attention. I said, "Annika, you can make things right with yourself and heaven when you live up to this commitment. You will see miracles happen." I told her that love and truth are the keys that will set her free.

Annika agreed to recite an affirmation of love—"Let me rise above with love"—every day and whenever she needed strength. It is a very simple affirmation, but it is very powerful.

A phrase was passed along by Annika's father, so I asked her, "What does s*lava bogu* mean? I hope I pronounced this correctly." There was complete silence for a moment, and I thought I had lost the overseas phone connection. Annika said, "Maudy, you just spoke Russian and you pronounced it very well!" I quickly responded that I did not speak Russian and that the words came from her father. She told me that the phrase means "God bless." She was in total awe, and so was I.

Her father told me that upon her return to the States, Annika would meet a man of prominence who was chosen for her by her father! Annika wanted to get married but had been hesitant because of her past. Now that she had dealt with her past and accepted love for herself, she was able to go forward.

One and a half years after our phone conversation, Annika called to tell me that she had married a surgeon and they were expecting their first child. She said it was hard to practice the spiritual law of love, but it was the phrase *slava bogu* that helped her move forward and make changes in her life. She had to hear these words from her father via a stranger across the ocean in order to get her life back on track.

Instructions from Heaven

John works the night shift at a local television station. He attended one of our presentations, sat attentively in the front row, and took voluminous notes in his notepad. Due to his work schedule, he wasn't able to stay for the entire presentation.

After my initial introduction to the attendees, someone named Joseph urged me to speak to John.

I went up to John, greeted him with a hug, and said, "Who is Joseph?" Tears immediately welled up in John's eyes. He held back his tears and said, "He is my dad, who has passed."

"Well, he is saying something in Creole, so bear with me as I pronounce it: *St. Crou.*" John acknowledged this is how the island of St. Croix, where his family originated, is pronounced in Creole.

Suddenly, his grandmother, who had also passed, joined in the conversation. She was making herself heard loud and clear. She stated she was born in the Gallos Bay area of St. Croix. She kept giving me a lot of messages for John, but I had difficulty trying to make out what she was saying. I started by asking him, "Is hospital in the name of her street?" By this time, John started to cry, and it was difficult for him to speak. He told me that he was thinking of building a hospital in his father's name on the island.

John explained that his dad always wanted his children to do business there as the opportunities were immense. The family has owned a lot of land on St. Croix for centuries, and they still own a fair share.

Joseph was very insistent that I tell John that he should build a church on the land in St. Croix. John's reply was, "Okay, a church. I'll do that."

It always amazes me how those who have passed clearly describe what they want to pass along and how necessary it is to assist you on your own life's journey! This is one of the best examples of people who have passed and are, in spirit, doing earthly work from heaven.

Rosa Parks and Coretta Scott King to the Rescue

A fantastic example of how those who have gone before us, related or not, can assist us on our life's journey focuses on Mindy. Suzy, a good friend of ours, set up a small presentation for us at her home. She asked her sister-in-law Mindy to attend, but it took her quite a while to accept. Mindy was not familiar with my work. Suzy confided that Mindy kept saying, "Good grief, girl. What have you gotten yourself into?"

Mindy finally decided to attend the presentation, but arrived late due to a previous engagement. Since Mindy had missed most of the general information at the beginning, we recapped some of the discussion. She admitted she was quite skeptical, but she listened intently.

Mindy's decision to attend was based on her fear that she had raised a "disease to please" child. She admitted she was a control fanatic and aware that she would encourage her daughter to always please others at the cost of neglecting herself.

Mindy wanted to stop a relationship that she felt would be harmful to her daughter. She was concerned that her daughter would marry this man and was afraid of the eventual outcome. I told her that when you let them go, you let them stay. What this means is that when you avoid controlling the lives of others, you actually keep them close. If you hold on too tight and continue to control them, you have a chance to be rejected. So when you let them go, they will continue to stay close to you. Mindy understood that the control issue was getting her down, and now was the time to let go.

While Mindy was talking to me, Mindy's mother-in-law was sending me a message through the angels' grapevine. The message was making me laugh because she said, "That would happen over my dead body!" She was already dead! I expressed this out loud and everyone laughed, which eased some of the tension.

I began to smell cinnamon buns and relayed this to Mindy. With tears in her eyes, she said, "While you were speaking, I could also smell the scent of cinnamon. My mother-in-law made the best homemade cinnamon buns in the world. I remembered her making them for breakfast, and the entire house smelled like cinnamon. Not one of her seven daughters learned to make those delicious buns!"

Mindy asked about her job, and her mother-in-law started to really get chatty and had a lot of messages to pass along. She said, "There is a situation that you need to take care of—and you can do it! There is also a change with your job." She continued to say that a person in a high place was going to offer her a very important position that involves something related to her current line of work, which was associated with the city council. Mindy's mother-in-law said, "You will be asked to be the leader or director of a job that would have great impact on the community. This job will be related to situations and things that Rosa Parks and Coretta Scott King faced. They will be assisting you on your journey."

At this point, the table lamp was flickering. I felt goose-bumps, which is my acknowledgement of spiritual confirmation. I also felt the presence of Rosa Parks and Coretta Scott King. The light kept flickering, so Suzy went to go find another bulb.

Mindy explained that she had been conducting multiculturalism trainings for a number of years, which included issues centered on racism, and was afraid that she was not ready to take on community issues. With reassurance from her mother-in-law, I congratulated Mindy and said, "I am honored to be in your presence. You are going to do great things." Mindy was in awe from the encouragement I had passed along, and so was everyone else.

By this time, the light had completely gone out, and Suzy was still rummaging around for a bulb. Once I started talking to another person, the light came back on all by itself, and stayed on for the rest of the night. I explained to Mindy that I honestly felt Mrs. King had visited and caused the lamp to flicker, and that she would have something to do in reference to Mrs. King.

The next day, Gail received an e-mail and phone call from a very excited Mindy. When she got to work that morning, she was asked to facilitate a community forum with a group of citizens about the naming of Martin Luther King, Jr. Street, which was scheduled for the following week.

We received another note from Mindy a few weeks later that stated she dealt with a difficult situation with the group of citizens.

From the time I was contacted to when I arrived at the town, the facts about the sentiment of factions in the community changed several times. The African-

American community was upset about several issues.
So by the time we arrived, it was pretty hairy.

In the past, I would have been on pins and needles.
Anxiety would have shown through my nonverbal com-
munication. This time, I was calm rather than nervous.
About a hundred people attended the meeting and it
went very well. I was humbled by the experience and
couldn't help to think that someone was assisting me and
the team as we conducted the meeting. I said, "Thank
you Jesus for blessing me." I know Mrs. King was with
me. We will be going back in a month, and I know that
I will be able to handle whatever may surface.

Thank you Maudy for the extraordinary
experience, and next time I will arrive on time!

Mindy has attended several presentations and admits that she still feels the assistance from Rosa Parks and Coretta Scott King.

I am always amazed at how fast some messages go into action. Sometimes the messages are faster than UPS or FedEx! This certainly was the case with Mindy.

Love Will Conquer All

Love can return to one's life when it is least expected, but you have to be aware and open to accept it. Betty was a bit apprehensive, but she came to a presentation at the urging of her daughter.

When it was Betty's turn to ask a question, she started to cry. Bob, her high school sweetheart and husband of thirty-four years, had passed away two years ago, and she was having difficulty getting her act together.

Bob had a neuromuscular disease that was progressively degenerative, and for the last fourteen years of their marriage, Betty was both mom and dad to the children, and worked full time in order to support the family. Betty stated it was a privilege to serve her family and had no regrets, except she now had difficulty finding herself. Her story was so moving that everyone at the presentation was in tears.

Gail and I explained the seven elements to Betty and emphasized, "Everything begins with you." She expressed that she had "skipped herself," had spent the last four years in therapy for depression, and was at her wits' end. She felt God had led her to this presentation and she was open to any and all messages intended for her so she could move forward.

Bob joined the conversation and thanked Betty for her incredible unending love and patience. He said he was bitter on earth, but not in heaven. He said he wanted Betty to go on with her life and that he would pick out a suitable partner for her. Betty started to cry again and Bob assured her they would meet again in heaven and always be together. By this time, the tissue box was nearly empty because everyone was so touched by what they just witnessed. Betty was beaming a beautiful smile.

The next day, Gail got a surprise call from a very happy Betty. Gail told me that she didn't know who it was because Betty wasn't crying. She went through an entire box of tissues during the presentation. This was definitely not the same person. She could hardly contain herself. She said that last night before she went to sleep, she felt her husband sit on the bed and place his arm on her arm in a very comforting way. Betty added that this was the first time in almost two years she had slept through the night.

Betty went to the psychologist the following week, and the doctor could not get over her new attitude and outlook on life. In fact, the psychologist was so impressed with her progress that he advised her that she no longer needed to have regular visits and to phase out all the medication that she had been dependent upon for four years. Betty stated she felt the veil of depression and mourning starting to leave her. She was ready to go on with her life.

When we saw Betty at another presentation nine months later, she was a new and refreshed person full of life. She had been talking to Ed, a former classmate, for few months, and they had been on a date. Ed had found her on an Internet registration of local high schools. They had gone on a date thirty-seven years ago when they were in high school, which Ed remembered but Betty didn't.

At the presentation, Betty wanted to know if Ed was the person that Bob had picked out for her because she was very comfortable with him. I did receive information from Bob at this presentation, and it was him urging Betty to get back into the dating scene. Bob had picked not one, but two men for Betty.

Bob wanted Betty to have great experiences in life; that is why Ed came into her life. This other man was also a very suitable option, but it was ultimately Betty's choice. She needed to look at her strength and focus on that and herself while taking things one day at a time.

She had dated both men, but it was rather clear through the messages that Ed was the one to get Betty out of her shell. Betty, through tears, expressed her thankfulness to Bob and added, "Chapter one of my life was terrific. I was blessed!" So even if thirty-seven years have passed, dating is always new and exciting! I always say nobody is perfect, but love is love from above.

To all of you who have faced a situation like Betty's, you have to look inward for that strength. In order to overcome depression and difficulties in life, each of you must learn to recognize your own strength, especially when it comes to letting go. You can make the choice to find the willpower to make the change for yourself.

Your Parents Are Your Parents, But Are Not

I come across many people who are not raised by their biological mother or father. This is important for everyone because there are many forms of blended families. What you must remember in this situation is that you are given a mother or father figure that you need to recognize. This is necessary because it is where true love actually comes from.

A child can be raised by a grandparent, aunt, sister, or someone who is not related. The true parents are the people where love comes from. The umbilical cord does not necessarily have to be attached to the parental figure. It is what I refer to as the invisible umbilical cord assigned by above. These children are chosen by God to be raised by whomever they were appointed to as family.

When I say "Your parents are your parents but are not," I mean that you were provided with someone who has loved you and provides parental care for you during their lifetime.

You were sent to earth to accomplish great things, regardless of your birth circumstances. Only look forward with great anticipation, knowing that you are special and have a very special purpose in life. It is where love comes from.

In my years of helping others, I have connected with many people who cannot go forward because of an abortion or relinquishing a child for adoption. The hurt is still rooted deep within the soul. Both circumstances deal with great emotional loss. However, it's their personal choice, which can affect their daily lives. I also have spoken to many adopted children who are searching for their birth parents.

I refer to abortions and miscarriages as voluntary and involuntary recalls. Both situations involve great emotional stress. Regardless of the circumstances, I am instructed to remind people to forgive themselves and to ask their higher power for forgiveness. The sixth element is forgiveness, which always begins with you. Without the forgiveness of oneself, one will continue to live in the past, unable to move forward and unable to love him or herself or others. This is when I go to work.

Reassurance for a Birth Mother

Jenny had reached a difficult point in her life and called me after a friend of a friend gave her my phone number. We went over many circumstances of her life, and she was telling me what took place in her life as far as children. I said, "I believe you mean two voluntary recalls and one child you placed for adoption." There was silence on the other end of the phone.

"Yes, that is correct. Who is giving you this message?" I said it was from her mother, who had passed many years before, and she was sad about the circumstances that surrounded the adoption, which had happened forty-seven years ago.

Jenny mentioned there had been abuse in her family, and because of it, none of her three sisters had children. One of the reasons she wanted to meet the child she had relinquished so long ago was because her entire family was childless. Jenny still had not forgiven herself and finally wanted to go forward. She continued, "There were very few people I ever trusted as a result of my childhood."

All of a sudden, another spirit joined the conversation and delivered a message. "Jenny," I said, "you did trust one person, and it was a priest."

"Oh my goodness, that is correct," she said. "He was very good to me. He is the priest I went to when I found out I was pregnant, and we spoke about adoption. He guided me through this."

I said, "This priest, Father William, wants you to go to your Bible. It has a note of encouragement that he wrote to you forty-seven years ago. He wants you to read it tonight." Jenny called me back that same evening and was crying. She found the note that she tucked away in that Bible but had not read it in years. It was a note of encouragement telling her that "heaven will take care of you and your child" and to go forward.

About six weeks after I first spoke with Jenny, she called me and said she had written to the agency where she had placed her daughter. The child she had relinquished had also written to this agency and wanted to meet her birth mother. Jenny was asked if she could come from California to South Carolina and meet her daughter. Jenny was very nervous about this meeting and asked if I could accompany her. Since Gail and I had a presentation in South Carolina that weekend, I agreed.

Many people who have relinquished a child or were adopted want to meet the child or parent because they usually feel a void at some point. This is fine as long as both parties are prepared to accept and respect what happens. Whether it is birth parents seeking children or adopted children seeking birth parents, the same is true for each: it is never what happens to you, but how you handle what has happened to you.

We must always be mindful that it might be a painful experience for the person searching for biological parents, but it is also a difficult situation for the adoptive parents. They are concerned about not having their child hurt. Circumstances of adoption vary from one person to another, and it is usually done for the well-being of the child and the person relinquishing the child.

We met at a restaurant in South Carolina, and our group consisted of Gail, myself, Jenny, Jewell, and Sandy, Jewell's adoptive mother. I was a bit amazed that Jenny actually looked like her adopted mom, not her birth mother.

At first, I could sense a little mother rivalry between Jenny and Sandy. I heard Jewell say, "My little girl." I knew Sandy was not comfortable and was thinking, "Why wasn't she able to take care of her? I have wondered for all these years."

Jenny was sharing parts of her life story and explained there was so much abuse in her family that it was difficult for her growing up, and patience was still an issue in her life. She said that all of her three sisters decided against having children because of the abuse. Jenny had not married, nor did she have any other children. She started her search for Jewell because she wanted to complete one chapter in her life.

Jewell was listening very quietly and intently to Jenny's words. Then this very wise young woman said, "Don't you realize that by placing me up for adoption you broke the cycle of abuse?" There was continued conversation, and I was very impressed with this young woman's observation. Jenny and Sandy were both astonished by Jewell's epiphany.

It was now my cue to pass along the messages being delivered from the grandmothers of Jenny and Sandy that "all will be well." I further explained to them your parents are your parents, but are not; your children are your children, but are not. Regardless of which mother biologically had this child, it was intended for Jewell to be raised in the family that was chosen for her. I know sometimes this is difficult to understand, but this is the way it is. It is how each of them handled what was placed in front of them, and it is this child. We are here for our own purpose, goal, and destiny.

We had a lovely visit, and as everyone was ready to leave the restaurant, I observed Jenny thanking Sandy for giving Jewell such a wonderful life and noting that she had turned out to be such a wonderful woman with a great head on her shoulders. Then Sandy said, "Each birthday I pray for you and ask God to bless you. Also, I want to thank you for giving me my daughter." The women embraced each other and asked Gail to take a picture of all three of them. It was such a fabulous sight to see. Everyone keeps in touch and is getting to know each other. This is the way it was intended to be.

Spiritual Escape to Get in Shape

Every day after feeding my cats and dogs, I go for a power-walk around the block for about fifteen minutes. This daily routine keeps the blood circulation going and energizes me in a variety of ways. It is my spiritual escape to get in shape and gives me the quality time to pray and meditate that I need before I start my day.

The fresh morning scent, the beautiful flowers, and the color of the leaves give me powerful inspiration, especially when I hear the birds sing. When you listen carefully, you can hear how the birds respond to each other. They carry on a bird conversation that makes me feel serene and joyous. The only busybodies I see are the squirrels. They seem always to be in a tizzy. They move so quickly that it is fascinating to see what they are going to do next.

I really enjoy my mornings and feel like each scene takes my breath away. Life is not measured by the breaths you take but what takes your breath away. When I am on these walks, my thoughts wander and I ponder. I often think to myself how awesome it is that the world is striving to preserve nature. I do have to chuckle as not everyone is as concerned for nature and don't clean up after their dogs. My walking trail becomes an obstacle course!

Sometimes we have to watch where we walk and be alert. This also relates to our daily life when we face life's challenges. It is necessary to be aware of how people can ambush us through conversations that may work against us. This can cause us stress and frustration. The aware phrase I share with people is "Don't let people's mess be your stress." This also applies to where you walk literally and figuratively. We all have to watch where we are going and avoid walking into a mess that can cause us stress.

I encounter many familiar faces on my morning walk. One of those individuals is Claire, who takes her cute little dog out every morning for a walk. I hadn't seen her for a while, and one morning I noticed Claire near her house in a pink robe and slippers. I waved and said "Hi! What a beautiful morning. How are you?" She was. Claire smiled and quietly said, "Just fine." It was nice to see her again, and I continued walking.

As I got closer to my house, I saw Jeanie and her four-year-old daughter Madison, whom my daughter often babysat. We exchanged hellos and Jeanie asked, "Do you always walk every morning?" I answered, "Yes, I enjoy starting my day this way and I keep my exercise going! I enjoy the fresh air and see neighbors I haven't seen for quite some time." Then Jeanie said, "Did you hear about what happened to my neighbor Claire?" I said, "No, but I did see her on my walk today. She was walking with her cute dog. I asked her how she was doing and she said, 'Just fine.'"

Jeanie said, "Well, that couldn't have happened because Claire passed away last week in her house."

At this point in the conversation, I became a little pale and said, "Are we talking about the same Claire and her dog?" Jeanie replied, "Yes, Claire passed away last Friday. She died of a heart attack!"

Jeanie looked at me and said, "You look like you've seen a ghost!" I answered, "I guess I have." Jeanie smiled and didn't realize what I was saying and how it affected me. My stomach was in a knot as I walked home!

As I stated before, I do not do well with spirit appearances. This particular experience was rather mild because Claire was still going about her business and routine. Therefore, my emotions were not shocked because I was focused upon my walk and enjoying the beauty of nature.

The reason I saw Claire is that during the forty days after a person dies and crosses over, their energy field is so strong that they can be anywhere they want to be as this is part of their transformation. They are allowed to visit their favorite places and go back where they once were. They can do what made them feel happy and visit those that they loved and say goodbye. When I saw Claire, both of us were going about our business and I was too busy to recognize she was actually in spirit. Claire was too busy with her own spiritual escape, which in turn got me out of shape. It was her way of saying, "Hi and goodbye." When I returned home from my walk, I reviewed this interesting scenario and prayed for Claire to have peace and finally rest.

Love in the Animal World

Love exists in many forms, which includes the love we have for our pets. When I receive messages from heaven, things are always very cryptic but very clear. I have often had the opportunity to see an animal that belonged to someone. Many times I will see a dog or a cat near someone who has passed. I'll describe the animal in detail to the person asking the question. They will know immediately if it was Fluffy the cat or Fido the dog. I always find it rather amusing, but rather nice to see that our animal friends stay with us always.

Gail and I were at a presentation and a young woman named Susan asked a question about her dad. She wanted to know how her dad was doing in heaven. I smiled because, as I've explained before, everyone lives with love, truth, and happiness in heaven.

The first message that came to me was someone was a heavy smoker. I said, "I am not sure if it is your dad, but did he smoke?" She said in a tear-filled voice, "Oh yes, and he smoked a lot!" Then suddenly the scenario of that message had changed and I saw a lot of deer around this man who had passed. The deer were showing this man where they were shot. They were not bleeding. I wasn't exactly sure why this was being presented to me, but I knew that this must be connected to his life. I asked Susan if her father was a hunter. She confirmed this all and became emotional.

Then Gail said, "Well, God loves animals too. After all, he had Noah gather animals, two by two, just before the great flood!" It's a good thing to have Gail next to me, reminding me of a story and bringing an interesting point to attention. God's love for animals is well expressed in the Bible, which allows us to recognize and understand that our love for animals is observed in heaven and how they should be treated here on earth.

I then received a message from Susan's grandmother Margaret. I asked Susan, "Who has pancreatic cancer?" She said, "I don't know."

I repeated it again, and Susan couldn't remember any-one with pancreatic cancer. I said, "Well, your grandmother is telling me to tell you, 'Tell her about Rose and Marie.'"

Susan started sobbing. I said, "Well, whoever they are, they want to say thank you!"

Susan finally said she was an animal rescue worker. Rose and Marie were her first rescued ferrets. Rose passed away from pancreatic cancer.

I looked at Gail in amazement and said, "Well, this is a first!" I had never received a message from animals to pass along to someone. We went from crying to laughing, which is necessary for the yin and the yang of life. It was a funny experience, but it was very healing and therapeutic to Susan, who has so much love for animals.

The moral of this story is that animals will never forget us. It is a very special and unique bond between human and animal. Your loved ones and animals walk beside you in heaven's landscape.

Everything is based upon love, truth, simplicity, and plain old common sense. I often say at presentations, "You can break criminal law or moral law, never heaven's law as in the law of love."

Will you make these choices here on earth? Will you allow yourself to learn about you? What will your life choice be? Will you reject or accept yourself?

We were loved before we were born and long before our parents, spouses, children, and friends loved us or hurt us. This is life's truth.

We are here on earth with love, for love, and by love. We are here for our own purpose, goal, and destiny. Once you realize that as truth, your life begins to be truthful and you will experience life being featherlight.

Love and Truth Is the Key that Will Set You Free
Love, Honor, Respect, Patience, Courage
Forgiveness and Belief
Seven elements of Heaven's Law
For us to live
We will overcome our grief when we can give
Ourselves … Love
What we do in the dark,
Will come out in the Light
The burden of our inner fight
Will be lifted
It's not how long you live—
But how you live
With Love and truth … the Key that will
    set you free!

On Love: Maudisms to Remember

A Maudism (or Coat Hanger) is a phrase to memorize and hang on to when you are facing difficult situations.

Rise Above with Love

....

When you let them go, you let them stay

....

Love Will Conquer All

....

Your Parents are your Parents, but are not…

....

Your Children are your Children, but are not…

....

You are here for your own goal, purpose and destiny

....

Love yourself first and then the world

....

Nobody is perfect, but love is from above

....

Don't let people's mess be your stress

TWO

Honor

Honor. To have honor is to first honor the gifts that are given to you. When you honor yourself, you learn to honor and recognize it in others.

You are sent into the world for a brief amount of time. You are chosen and sent to learn how to love yourself, honor and respect yourself, forgive yourself, heal yourself and others, remove fear and bring peace, faith, and love to yourself first, and then to others. It is necessary to be aware of the fact that it is not about how long you live, but how you live.

We are bombarded with so much misery and hardship in our society and in times of crisis that our hearts get numb. We often feel paralyzed because we are overloaded. We tend to be restless when we are waiting for that mysterious moment to have our prayers answered and problems solved. It is at this time that we become anxious, angry, and impatient. This is when you need to focus on the seven elements and honor yourself and take care of you first.

Honoring Yourself

Personally, I honor myself during Lent, the forty-day period between Ash Wednesday and Easter Sunday. I give up what I love to do most, which is to pass along goodwill and angel whispers. In this silent time, I pray and meditate to energize myself. I don't even speak with Gail, who is very busy during this period talking with and comforting people in need.

When you cross my path, it is my mission to help you with your heavenly résumé and let you know what your mission is here on earth. Being a mystic, I cannot ask the loved ones in heaven questions—I can only hear the information. I have the gift to recognize people and their life journey; to let them know what is documented in their personal database. My gift of prophecy allows people to look forward to positive news. When I deliver your message, I am not the miracle worker who makes it come to pass—it is you! I am only a messenger. You are the one who will experience your own miracle through your own personal choice.

In honoring ourselves, we must build up our heavenly résumé by doing good here on earth. We accomplish this by living the intangible gifts of love, honor, respect, patience, courage, forgiveness, and belief. My mission is to help you understand your mission so you can spend your life doing good here on earth and have a good résumé. I present the choices to you to help you checkmark your own personal box of seven elements, but each person has to make the individual choice to move forward.

Set Your Timer

We need to go through our grieving and mourning process when our loved ones pass away. It is very important to take our time to cry, scream, be angry, and be sad. Set your timer for about ten minutes and let go of all the emotions. There's nothing wrong with getting it all out! When the timer goes off, pick yourself back up. Inhale and exhale, and do something nice for you. This technique can help with many strong emotions. You need to get your feelings out, but not dwell on them. Honor yourself by expressing your feelings and moving on. A kite always rises against the wind when we learn to look at our strength.

Children who have lost loved ones or pets also need to go through the same process. I've sent animal-shaped kitchen timers to many children throughout the years. I tell them to set the timer and scream, cry, and be angry. When the timer goes off, they are to breathe and let go of the sad and angry feelings. I also have sent "hug me" pillows to children. I instruct them to punch the pillow when they were mad or squeeze them for love. I told them to imagine that it might be the loved one they lost whom they were hugging. It's so cool to see the child happy when Grandma from heaven is sharing a story and the child confirms this. The children feel comfortable with this and call me their walkie-talkie for heaven.

When we reflect and have flashbacks, we can fall back in a slight depression. Just be alert and don't let this control you. Repeat this ritual of setting your timer, and the pain will echo away. It takes positive effort to see positive results.

Rembember, our loved ones never leave us. In order to keep a connection with them, we need to deal with our emotions. When we can't let go of the sad emotions, our loved ones will not be able to connect with us through the portals of our dreams. By honoring ourselves and letting go of negative feelings, we bring more to ourselves and open ourselves to everything around us.

During the Forty Days after Passing

When we die, our souls are evaluated to understand how we lived here on earth when we go from human into spirit. What did we do for others and ourselves? Were we kind to others and ourselves? For many people, life is what we do to ourselves rather than for ourselves, which escalates into negative life choices.

When a person dies, I honor their passing for forty days because this is a special time between the soul and the higher power. Therefore, I honor the one who has passed and will not be able to deliver messages to the family members.

The energy field within this time frame becomes extremely strong for our loved ones who have passed. The deceased will be able to let their presence be known and show signs they are around us. During this time, you may experience powerful, supernatural occurrences. You might experience lights flickering or the radio or television turning on or off by itself. Many very interesting and odd things happen during this time frame that will give you goosebumps. When this happens, it is angelic confirmation that your loved one is near.

On the day of my mother's funeral, I was standing in the kitchen and the door was open. A little sparrow flew into the house. I screamed because I had to duck to avoid a collision with this bird. I was afraid that it would fly into my hair, and that would be a different way of feeling goosebumps. I certainly wanted to avoid that! The sad emotions were immediately replaced by shock and then great laughter. I knew Mom was giving me signs to recognize the joy of her being there and watching me.

During this forty-day time frame, you may also experience dreams with your loved ones. Shortly after Gail's dad passed in December 2008, I had a dream about Mr.

Hunt. He smiled at me and said, "Still livin'." This was funny because each time I would visit with him at Gail's house, I'd ask how he was and he'd answer, "Still livin'!" I know that this was an acknowledgement from him and his heavenly arrival.

Gail had a dream of her dad after he had passed. He was in the hospital and was getting out of bed and dressed. He said hello and that he was getting ready for work. This was a very clear answer to Gail to let her know that her dad is doing his earthly work from heaven.

Back on Track through Faith

One Sunday afternoon, we were invited to the home of Jim Smith for a presentation. We had met Jim briefly at a presentation at his daughter's home. He was a skeptic and hadn't attended any of the presentations with his wife and two daughters. Because he observed major changes in their lives, he made the decision to open up his home to us.

Gail and I were so pleased that so many men showed up at the presentation at Jim's house because this would be a definite boost for him and his confidence. When it was time to ask questions, Jim expressed concerns that dealt with his religious beliefs and how he had abandoned them long ago due to circumstances in his life.

The biggest circumstance was that he was adopted. He had not fully dealt with those feelings, and it caused him much hurt, especially when his dad passed away the previous year. His dad, Jack, was in his eighties and his best friend. Jim never met his biological father, nor had he adequately dealt with his inner feelings.

Jim was listening intently as I was explaining the theory that your parents are your parents, but are not, as I detailed in the previous chapter. I explained that you are here for your own goal, purpose, and destiny. As I was talking, I was listening to angel information from Jack, Jim's father.

Jack was letting me know how they used to throw stones at the lake and watch them skip across the water. When this was brought to the attention of Jim, he and his wife and daughters became very emotional. Everyone was crying because they recognized exactly what Grandpa was saying.

While talking to Jim, I suddenly heard a Phil Collins song. I looked at Gail and said out loud "Phil Collins," and Gail said, "Genesis. It is Genesis in the Bible."

Jim immediately said, "What does that have to do with anything?" As he was talking, I saw a digital clock in my mind's eye, which said 9:12. I told Jim, "You have a note in your Bible, a message from your father, and it is in Genesis. Oh by the way, read Genesis, chapter 9, verse 12." Jim was silent, but took note of the information that I was receiving from his father.

Then I said, "Jim, your father is asking why you haven't been praying? What does your father mean with honoring the Bible?"

Jim looked like he was in shock and responded, "I haven't picked up the Bible in forty years!" At this point, it was too emotional for Jim to go on, and I left him with the message he needed to hear.

Jim called a few days later and was so excited. He choked up during the conversation because he found a handwritten note from his dad that had been tucked away in his Bible for forty years. It was in Genesis, and he read the chapter and verse that I had mentioned. He felt his dad was conveying a personal message through this passage. Jim was grateful for this note from his dad, and the reasons for leaving his faith were no longer relevant.

He told us he was a changed man as a result of this encounter and expressed his deepest gratitude. He is now enjoying life with his wife, children, and grandchildren. His wife and daughters later shared that the depression and burden that he was carrying for all these years were visibly lifted and he was a new man.

With Jim, it was necessary to restructure his faith by honoring his dad and the Bible. For me as a messenger, it was an honor to bring honor to the attention of Jim.

Cellphone from Heaven

The way our loved ones connect with us is always obvious to me. The following story is an example of how strongly our loved ones want to let us know of their presence.

Mr. Weiss is a sixty-six-year-old man from Belgium. He was married for forty years to his wife Anna. They shared everything and couldn't live without each other. Mr. Weiss and his wife wanted to downsize and move from their house to a smaller apartment. Anna picked out new curtains, carpet, and furniture and was excited about the interior decor in the new apartment. But Anna was diagnosed with breast cancer and admitted to the hospital before they could finish all the renovations to the apartment. It wasn't very long before she lost her battle with cancer.

Mr. Weiss was very lonely and sad. He wrote me an e-mail and asked, "Maudy, I moved into our new apartment and want to know if Anna likes the house. Does she like how I finished the interior design?" He continued to explain that something very awkward happened in the new apartment and wanted my interpretation of what took place.

When Anna was admitted to the hospital, he gave her a cell phone. He was at the hospital day and night, but felt it was good for her to have a phone. No one knew her number besides him and their children.

About six months after her death, the strangest thing happened. He said, "I was talking to her like she was here, in front of her picture, and I said, 'Anna, if you like it up there, please let me know. I will manage down here, but please give me a sign.'"

Then he said, "Maudy, I heard her cell phone ring three times and then it was completely silent. Now, is this really a sign from her?"

I immediately e-mailed him back and said yes, it definitely was a call from heaven. Anna also gave me a message for her husband: "I am home and like my new home. It was already furnished. Your final touch in our house was my choice." So, did she like it? You bet she did!

Mr. Weiss' questions were answered and he understood. By honoring his wife with continuing to refurbish the house, she assisted him with the decisions.

Our loved ones can actually dial our number and make the call to let us know that they can hear us without being on the phone. How cool is that?

Honor to Carry Your Cross

I often talk about life training during presentations and seminars. It means that experiencing any form of hardship contributes to our life training. Whether it's dealing with the loss of our loved ones or something in our personal life that causes mental aches and pains, it's all a big part of helping us learn how to overcome and get us where we need to be. Of course, it is the hardest pain to bear our own cross, but by looking at our strength, we can honor ourselves and allow for peace to grow within us.

God always puts people on our path to help us take up that cross. Sometimes you can recognize others going through their struggles and you are called to help them. Healing comes from assisting others who are in need of healing. It takes courage, willpower, and self-love to make this positive choice. Let me share with you my story of how I am honored to carry my cross.

People often ask me, "Maudy, with your gift, do you know anything for yourself or your family?" I reply by saying, "My gift is for others, so no, many times I don't know things for myself or my family." Since gifted people are never prophets in their own homes, it's often ignored anyway. When heaven allows me to know, it's up to me to share or to keep myself in silence.

As an angel whisperer, I hear for others and relay the messages. My own messages come through conversations with other people, usually during presentations. I need to recognize the message through clarity of mind and understand I will learn what I need to know. I am protected from possible personal emotions that could work against me so I will be able to continue doing heavenly work here on earth and won't be distracted. The saying comes to mind: "What you don't know cannot hurt or harm you."

My oldest daughter, Priscilla, called me from her workplace and asked if I could talk to her friend. "Sure," I said, "Put her on the phone!" Rene said, "I heard so much about you and was wondering if you could help me with some things I'm going through?"

I first explained to Rene how my gift works and she was very excited; she had pencil and paper ready and was writing things down as I was relaying the messages. I could hear Rene becoming emotional when she recognized the past scenarios of herself and her family. Then I heard through angel whispers about a friend of hers. I told her, "Rene, you will have to be strong because a friend will need your help. She's very close to you and you can't fall apart. I will already pray for her and you. I'm not sure what is going on, but what I was told was that she will be very sick. It could be cancer or other health problems. This message is not negative but heaven is requesting your help and prayers. Just be strong and be there for her, okay?" Rene replied, "Yes, I will!" as she thanked me for talking to her.

My daughter called me later that day to let me know that Rene was a little overwhelmed, but that she liked all the good news. Four months later, I was happy to hear that many things came to pass for Rene.

Five months after talking to Rene, my daughter Priscilla got married. A month after the wedding, my daughter was diagnosed with cancer. The unexpected hardship for Rene's friend was for my daughter.

Life can be a surprise or an ambush, and this was life's ambush! I knew this experience would be a big part of our life training. When you first hear the news, you become somewhat numb. I didn't want to give myself time to react but to act. Everything happened so fast after this news.

My daughter had a rapid-growing form of cancer so she was scheduled for surgery shortly after the diagnosis. From there, she had to undergo chemo and radiation. We all went through many emotional scenarios during this time.

My daughters and I all have long hair, so before Priscilla started her chemo treatments, she decided to cut her hair very short so it wouldn't be as hard and traumatic when she would lose it. My youngest daughter, Deanna, works at a spa and hair salon. She spoke to her boss, Sheila, who was very supportive and understanding when Priscilla came in for her haircut.

Deanna sat in the chair to Priscilla's left and I was sitting in the chair to her right. My husband was also there to provide moral support. The first locks came off as we were holding hands. Sheila stopped cutting Priscilla's hair and started preparing Deanna and me for our haircuts. Priscilla screamed, "What are you both doing? No, Mom!" Deanna and I answered, "You think we were going to let you go through this on your own? Heck NO! If you can cut your hair, then we can too!"

We turned this difficult time into laughter with tears streaming down our faces. It was an intense time, but it was also a time of big love and honor for Priscilla and the battle ahead of her. The hair that was cut from the three of us was donated to the Locks of Love Foundation.

The time after that became an emotional roller coaster even more. Going through this experience you just do what you have to do. Many people will recognize themselves in these situations and can reflect and identify their own story. I needed to live what was embedded in me and that was to let go and let God. Living in what I have learned was looking at my strength.

Strength is a powerful word we usually forget we have in us when going through hardships. It is okay to mourn and grieve. It is okay to cry for all that needs to be cried for. Taking time for yourself is very important even though it's hard when time is living you. After attending to my daughter from early morning to the late evening hours while she was dealing with chemo treatments, my alone time was on the drive home when I'd let my emotions go. I would turn up the radio or sing my own songs real loud. I know I had a silent audience of my loved ones in heaven. I'm sure they had a ball hearing me sing. My favorite song was "Let It Be" by the Beatles. I sang this song over and over again. I turned the song into prayer, and by repeating it over and over, I learned to keep my strength!

Learn to Own Your Pain

All of Priscilla's friends, including her boss, pulled together and were at her side from the beginning to this day where she is now CANCER FREE! We learned to own our pain throughout this battle with the support of those who were there to called to minister to us, guide us, teach us, and help heal us. My daughter is now assisting others as a traveler through their lives giving guidance, comfort, and her love. The choice of sharing life's struggles can become a service for others, where courage, hope, faith, honor, and most importantly love surfaces!

I asked Priscilla if she could share her thoughts with the readers. Without hesitation, she wrote this story and I am grateful and proud of her to share it with you. I hope my daughter's view and thoughts will strengthen and empower you.

One of the best days of my life was my wedding day. I was looking forward to seeing my family, which I hadn't seen in many years. They were coming to the wedding from all corners of the world. I was excited to finally start my life after some crazy detours. I imagined a future with children possibly in the picture and continuing to focus on my passion to rescue animals. I was finally on the right path, so I thought.

A few weeks after our honeymoon, I found a dreaded lump in my breast. You know the story; you never think it would happen to you. No one ever does. I went over my options with the doctor about surgery, chemo, radiation, and how I was going to afford this. It was so much to take in. Was I even physically and mentally strong enough to go through this? I couldn't stop thinking about the unknown pain I was about to go through, about the changes that my body was going to experience. But who wants to hear all that? I'd rather tell you the positives!

I appreciated every second of the day that I had my family, friends, and animal children supporting me. I honored myself by accepting what's happening and putting a positive spin on it. There were days that I didn't even recognize the woman looking back at me in the mirror. This woman I was looking at had no hair, was heavier due to steroids, looked tired and worn with a pale face. This was not my face; this was not me. However, if you look hard enough behind these eyes, there is a stronger woman now. A woman who feels the need to do something more by making a difference in this world, whatever that may be. Life is what you make of it!

We all have been given gifts, and one of them is making choices. You have the ability to choose how you deal with life's challenges. Sure, there were days where I wanted to scream, cry, and ask, "Why is this happening to me?" And I did! I have learned that the day you stop and ask why and start working on making things better is the day you have beaten one of your biggest obstacles. My best friend, Rene, reminded me what my mom had told her long before I was ever diagnosed. Mom had told her someone close to her would go through cancer and would need her help.

We both cried, realizing that person my mom told her about was me. My mom had no idea she was talking about her own daughter at that time. My mom often tells me that had she known, she probably wouldn't have handled it as well as she did.

During one of my chemo treatments, I was listening to a conversation of one of the other patients. It brought so much more into perspective. The patient was a middle-aged woman who was sitting a couple recliners away from me with IVs in her arm as well. She was talking with the nurse about only having a few months to live and about her daughter who was newly pregnant with her first child. I overheard the nurse, who was a bit choked up, say, "I'm sure you'll be looking down on your daughter and watching over her and her newborn." The patient gave a little smile and replied proudly, "I'm just excited I get to meet the baby before anyone else when I get to heaven." She was beaming with joy as she continued to talk about it more with the nurse who had tears in her eyes and was wearing a big smile. I thought to myself, what an amazing woman!

I thank God every day for my rocks in my life: my husband, animal children, friends, and family. This journey would have been a lot harder without a good support group. I hope you can take away from my story and to look at each challenge in life, no matter how big or small, as another opportunity. Maybe you can see this as an opportunity to showcase your ability to shine. Be the light when it gets dark!

Face Life and Embrace Life

Faith eliminates fear and creates strength and confidence. "When you turn to Faith, Fear will disappear." This is a Maudism that I remind people to memorize to get through the difficult days. We need to learn to have Faith embedded in us, because when we face life challenges, it can wound us and disturb our life routine. At some point, we come to appreciate our daily routine. We can only miss it when a great challenge takes place. Living through life's trauma is to face it and embrace it—this way, the healing factor can begin. Resisting life's hardship by turning to stress, frustration, and depression can cause us emotional harm. Remember, our minds have a powerful energy, and it can break you or make you. Showing resistance in challenging situations can block our healing. We need to convert negative thoughts or avoid them, as this can become destructive. Allowing positive thoughts, supported through prayer can convert this negative energy into the power of positive thinking!

Angels Around Us

Angels around us are the links to get us where we need to be. They can sometimes appear in a fellow traveler through our lives or a distant guide as in the strangers that have been put on our path. I have recognized them as the "positive pop ups," the unexpected spiritual guides. The spiritual guides appointed to you remind you to hold on to faith and that you cannot lose trust or distrust. They will reaffirm their commitment to you by your commitment to yourself. God gives you people who hold you, help you stay strong, and keep you from wandering off. In times of hardship, we can sometimes count only a few people to be there for us. Sometimes it's our family, but other times our distant friends take on the role of close family and become the angels around us!

Recognize the angels around you and let them lead you to your path of healing. You will learn to heal yourself and assist the person who is in need of healing. Sharing your struggle then becomes a service and offers courage and hope for others. Sometimes we are appointed by heaven to be the mission first, before we can serve the mission. When you guide, you teach, when you teach, you speak; when you speak you learn to listen to your own angel whispers. When we understand that love and faith will see us through, we will overcome any degree of hardship and embrace the blessings to pay it forward!

This is how to honor the cross you carried throughout your life!

Life is a Gift
Heaven is watching us—every step we take
Move we make and thought we create
We are here on earth with Love and for Love
Angels descending from above … will help us
    with our choices
When we listen to the Angel Voices

They will make hardship stop…
*   and lift our spirits up*
Life is simplicity and common sense
Life is what we allow
Life is to live in the now
Life is a Gift, that needs to be lived

On Honor: Maudisms to Remember

A Maudism (or Coat Hanger) is a phrase to memorize and hang on to when you are facing difficult situations.

It's not about how long you live, but how you live.
....
Set Your Timer
....
A kite always rises against the wind
....
Face Life and Embrace Life
....
It takes positive effort to see positive results
....
Let go and Let God
....
Turn to Faith and fear will disappear

THREE

Respect

Respect comes in many forms, but it begins with you. Respect is believing you are special no matter what, as well as recognizing the deeper value in people.

Living with respect comes in many forms. Respect for life comes from the way we live. People often neglect self-respect when they get the disease to please—this is when someone is always trying to please others and forgets about him or herself.

When we cannot deal with situations in life, we drink, smoke, shop, or eat (or don't eat) because of defeat. We might even want to do something we can hide behind so we don't have to face harsh reality. We get sidetracked and lose direction in life. An escalation or chain reaction of negative emotions can take place. Confusion, uncertainty, insecurity, stress, frustration, and depression are just a few things that can throw us off track and into a downward spiral. Our mental frustrations can also affect us physically, so we can literally be "worried sick."

One Rough and Tough Cookie

People often come to presentations with a skeptical attitude. I often explain that I welcome their curiosity because it demonstrates an open mind. However, some people are unwilling to ask a question during the personal encounter portion, and I wonder why they even bother to come. This is, however, fine with me, as I can only give the light when it is asked for.

When I present people with choices, it is usually the stubborn people who put up a defense, no matter how many positive options are relayed. In my mind, I pray, "Dear Lord, please put your arms over my shoulders and your hand over my mouth even as I am facing these rough and tough cookies!"

Heaven gives me a quick personal-life background check when I'm dealing with difficult people so I can understand their behavior. At this point, I realize I have to tap into a different way of reaching the person and present them with choices. I tap into tremendous patience because this category of people has lost love and honor along their personal life journey.

When I need to bring respect to a person's attention, it is usually to the individuals who deal with turmoil and turbulence within themselves and others.

Lucy, a twenty-three-year-old woman, attended a presentation and exhibited negative body language. Gail and I recognized she really did not want to be here.

I asked Lucy, "What do you want to do in life?"

"Nothing."

"Do you want to work?"

"No."

"Where do you live?"

"With my parents, husband, and sister."

"Don't you want to work?"

"No!"

By this time, I was getting pretty annoyed with this woman's one-word answers. I needed to get her interested in life and herself, so I said to her, "Well, you'll get depressed and grow old quickly if you don't work."

Lucy's sister chimed in and said, "Maudy, I offered Lucy a job to work with me at the day care. We needed help but she doesn't want to work or work with children. She doesn't like them."

Lucy was still only giving me a blank stare. I continued my questioning, "Do you want children?"

"No!"

"Why did you reject the offer to work with children?"

"I don't like children," Lucy answered.

I was still in a state of amazement with this person's one-word answers and negativity. However, I knew I had to leave her with her own thoughts and move on. It was a bit of a disruption, and I was ready to go to the next person in the presentation.

During the rest of the presentation, Lucy's aunt, who had passed away, was giving me information through the angels' grapevine. I was told that this young woman lost respect for herself and life. It was very important to give this woman information about how lack of respect would lead to depression and self-destruction.

As a positive mystic messenger, I had to blast Lucy with the strategy of love. This way the strict, strong, and stern words would be gently received and she would not turn away. With the help from her aunt and heaven, we would get through to her in one way or another.

I later went back said "Congratulations" to Lucy and gave her a hug at the end. At first, she did not understand, but then her eyes filled up with tears. Through heaven's network, I heard she was going to get pregnant, and the baby would bring respect to her world.

I turned to the group and gave everyone a better understanding of how heaven works and that we are not to mess with it in any way or form.

Just before we were about to leave, Lucy came up to me with tears in her eyes and asked, "Was my aunt giving you all of this information?"

"Yes," I said

"I can work with my sister at the day care with the children," she said with enthusiasm, and then she hugged me. I know that after listening to the entire group of people, and especially her father's story, she might be able to recognize the love and respect of life and correct her life accordingly. Her father attended the presentation and received an apology through angel whispers from a person who had passed and had abused him when he was a child.

Gail told me at the end of the presentation, "Maudy, that was a very rough and tough cookie that was starting to crumble!"

I smiled because my mission was accomplished. My prayer for Lucy was for heaven to help her not to neglect self-respect.

We always need to maintain respect for ourselves. Once you read this next story, perhaps you may see your own life scenario and will want to think and do things differently. This will help you make changes and let life work with you and for you.

Carly's Disease to Please

I recently met a woman named Carly at a presentation. The person in front of me was very fragile in appearance and very thin. She looked anorexic.

Carly grew up with always being there for others, always helping out and serving people. It was difficult for her to say no to her family and friends. She definitely had a very strong case of the disease to please because she always put other people first. She was afraid of what they would say or do if she said no. She expressed to me that she was depressed and asked, "Maudy, I feel like nobody is here for me. When will it be my time to enjoy life?"

I explained to her that we can be here for others, but we first need to be here for ourselves. Gail always gives the explanation at presentations that when you are on an airplane, the flight attendant teaches us to use the oxygen mask first on ourselves before you assist others, even if you are traveling with a small child or elderly person. You need to breathe first before you help others to breathe.

In life, it is very important to take care of yourself first. This is not a selfish act. You must first take time for you to avoid getting sick, losing weight, or gaining weight.

The disease to please is a negative pattern that creates fear. A person is plagued by fear of what people will think and do. When we allow people to take advantage of us, we lose self-respect. The following concept would have helped Carly and changed her life if she had recognized that you should never neglect self-respect.

I often mention that it is not wise to think or speak for others. Never assume anything. The best choice to make is to learn to be in control of yourself, which starts with your mind. When you get to this point, you are in charge of your life. I said this to Carly and asked her, "Is this hard for you to do?" There was silence for a few seconds, and she said "I will work on it."

As I explained to Carly, you can accomplish anything you put into your mind. It takes a lot of practice, but you can make it happen with constant maintenance and positive reinforcement.

Remember to make changes within yourself and set aside quality time for yourself. Say no to people who expect things from you. Lose that disease to please mindset and be in charge and control of you! Remind yourself of the three Cs = Control, Charge, Choice. Say it and mean it! You are in control, in charge, and in choice of your own life!

After a couple of months, we heard from Carly, who shared the good news that she is now able to say no and that she conquered herself by making changes. She told us it wasn't easy, but she has pulled back from people who emotionally drain her and is also physically doing better.

It takes self-love and willpower to keep our self-respect. As with Carly's cause and effect, everything is possible! Positive effort will show positive results.

Self-Control

Negative or positive, our own life's escalation is living up to our own expectations. Once we make a commitment to ourselves, it is a big step to self-discipline. Once we recognize this and control this, we have come a long way.

The source of the negative escalation is often caused by not seeing things progress in life. The weight on your shoulders is what you have carried from your past into the present. We have the tendency to break ourselves down when we can't deal with our emotions. This defeat makes it easier for people to take away our love, honor, and respect.

When we are constantly tempted, distracted, and disillusioned by the here and now wants, we don't see the true importance of life. Wants, not needs, can fracture your life. The best way to incorporate self-respect into your life is to use common sense to simplify your life.

Heavenly Health Plan

One of the major questions I always get, whether over the phone or at presentations, is about weight. This of course ties into self-control, how we eat, and how we take care of our body.

People sometimes forget that respect comes in this form. However, it is one of the key factors that ties in to our well-being. To live consciously is to maintain control. When people do not have self-respect in their personal behavior, their life patterns drastically change.

All the self-help and self-realization books that have been brought to your attention by others can be messages for you. These books give you the tools to help you move forward. This will help and remind you about the simplicity and common sense of life. Many teachers deliver these positive messages, just as they did centuries ago. Sometimes messages of simplicity can be expensive when we invest more in the teachers and do not recognize that this investment was actually to be an investment in ourselves. We'll give you the choice to invest in yourself in this chapter. Your mind has a powerful energy, therefore, this information will also help strengthen your body's defenses that starts by protecting your mind. It will also provide immunity from outside influences, which are daily distractions and temptations that challenge our sensitivity and vulnerability.

Many people start off the new year with resolutions that usually include new diets, exercises, programs, and other things to improve life. These resolutions are often restarted every year because we couldn't live up to our commitment. The engine of willpower got our motivation motor running and it broke down somewhere down the road. To prevent this from happening, we have the best teachers giving us guidance. All it takes is self-love, a dose of willpower, and the discipline of faith to help us maintain our self-respect.

With the diet comes the workout. The stair-step will be your positive life of evolving and revolving stairways. You need to create new patterns and habits for your life.

The treadmill will be your walk for life. Place one foot in front of the other, one step at a time. Push-ups will help you regain your willpower to give you the push in life and for life and not to allow people to push you around. Your mindset will be "I can and I will."

Sit-ups will help you strengthen your backbone so you can be strong and prevent people from breaking you down. Your mindset will be "I will say no," and you will lose the disease to please. Find your favorite happy music, turn it up, just dance, and be you! This will create joy, happiness, and peace.

The universe is watching you and will guide you with this exercise and new diet. It is your choice to be you and to follow through. This new health regimen will be easy on you. With all the upcoming birthdays our bodies will let us know what we are able to do or not do so we can go from tae-bo to tai chi. There's nothing wrong with that since we must face and embrace life, own it, and have peace with it. Just keep on moving forward, moving up, and moving on!

Recipe for Mind and Soul

Food is an important aspect to a healthy lifestyle. Here's a recipe to keep in mind:

Love as food coloring for self-love
Honor to present this dish created by you
Respect as an important dish to your life
Patience to prepare and make this dish
Courage to create this recipe with willpower
Forgiveness when you have put too
*   much pepper into your life's dish*
Belief is when your dish will be served

When you taste this dish and it's lacking spice, you might recognize that you need to spiritually kick it up a notch, to borrow a phrase from Emeril Lagasse. Add a few other acceptances of life ingredients to the mixture to create the perfect dish. Feeding the soul is feeding the body when you use the correct ingredients. It's all about preventing, preparing, and praying.

Before consuming this dish, add meditation and prayer as this becomes your discipline of the moment and of the day. This recipe will give fulfillment and helps with the digesting process to make life featherlight.

Your weight, as in the life baggage you carry around with you, will be lighter when you are able to let go and let God. The miracles of life take place when you face and embrace your past.

The universe, God, and angels can protect you from the outside world but cannot protect you from yourself. Be aware and become the ever vigilant chef so you can create your own masterpiece—you!

Gail's Perspective: Respect in All Aspects of Life

As the coauthor and Maudy's friend, I have observed that during presentations, that of all the elements, I think respect might be one of the most important—and perhaps one of the least understood. I also do part of the teaching at each presentation with Maudy. This is why I do the comfort talks during the year and during Lent, whenever is needed. As with all the elements, respect begins with the self first. In other words, respect yourself first, then the world.

Beginning with the self first is imperative in order to understand how respect works. When we say respect ourselves first, then the world...we mean respect for self, life, animals, people around us, our family and friends. This of course, is all for the good of leading a life where love, honor, respect come first, and will allow you to live life peacefully.

For a great majority, Maudy is the person that heaven has placed in front of them, so that they can recognize their own self-respect, and check mark that box for their heavenly resume. After all, this is what life is...we are working on our "heavenly résumé," here on earth.

Common Sense and Respect

For some individuals, common sense and respect seem to be on the opposite ends of the spectrum. Over the course of three and a half years, Susan, a thirty-eight-year-old businesswoman came to several presentations. Her question to Maudy was usually, "What about my relationship?"

The first time Susan came, she was in tears, and was telling Maudy about her recent relationship. The angel whisper being delivered by her great-grandmother to Maudy was: "Susan, the man you are with is tied up." It was obvious that Susan knew exactly what Maudy meant, although, the other participants in this group were not fully aware of what was going on. Maudy and Susan's eyes met, and she knew exactly what was being said and understood the implications.

Then Susan, said out loud to Maudy and the group: "Yes, he's separated, and has four children." But she felt that this was the one for her, and he said he was in love with her.

The second time we met Susan, again … the tears … with the same question. Maudy asked her about the man and said: "Well, how is that working for you?"

Susan indicated that things were working out, but she started questioning his love for her. The angel whispers being delivered to Maudy indicated that he was not totally truthful to her. When Susan heard this, she said she would look into it. It was very obvious to all of us that she was still in love with him so she had to decide what she wanted to do.

At this point, her great-grandmother was delivering angel whispers to Maudy—about this wonderful man that she was going to meet and how she had a lot to look forward to. Susan said she wasn't interested yet. Maudy said, okay, then let's just move forward. This is where

Maudy stopped and just looked at Susan, and we went to the next person in the group.

On the way home from this presentation, Maudy and I were talking about how, at that point, common sense went out the window—and perhaps the blinds were shut because she did not want to see what was actually happening.

The third time we saw Susan, yes, you guessed it...the same question came up: "What about my relationship?" Maudy asked her, "What happened to the individual that you were dating?" Her answer was: "Well, he went back to his wife, then divorced her and married someone else!" So, again with great-grandmother's help...the message that was delivered was: "Please look for someone that is not tied up." She laughed and looked at us, and said "I understand."

This is a sign of a person who, indeed, has a pattern of seeking out people who are not single and are tied up with other people. Again, this is a common-sense issue of lack of self-respect.

During this same encounter, great-grandmother was rather chatty and the messages kept coming and she was very specific, and said: "Susan, the best is yet to come. I have picked someone out for you, since you did not do such a great job for you. You will meet him at a fundraising event. Please give him a chance." So, we breathed a silent sigh of relief. Hopefully, Susan will listen to this great heavenly message, and change her lifestyle, so that respect will become her...and happiness is hers.

Missing Respect for Loved Ones

Sometimes, we miss respect for those that heaven has placed in our lives. Maudy and I met Mary, who was introduced by a mutual friend, at a coffee shop. Mary wanted one of our books and also wanted to come to a presentation. Her manner during the entire conversation was that of a person totally preoccupied by other things, and angry at the world for her particular circumstance.

Since Maudy and I had another appointment, we could only spend about thirty minutes with Mary, but invited her to a presentation the following evening.

Mary arrived about fifteen minutes late that evening and appeared to be very rushed and rather flustered. We were actually in the middle of the group presentation. Then, when we proceeded to the personal encounter time, and when it came time for Mary to ask her question, she blurted out that she was very angry with her mother, who had passed about one year ago, and could not get her life to-gether. She said, "My mother never loved me and was angry with me most of my life. I wasn't pleasant to her. How is she?"

Mary's Mom, Elizabeth came through and said: "Please forgive me." Mary's answer was, "I am not sure if I can." Everyone looked around at each other, then fixed their eyes on Mary. Maudy continued and said to Mary, in a very determined tone of voice, "Mary, your mother Elizabeth is asking for forgiveness. Do you forgive her?" Finally, she said, "Yes, I forgive her."

Further, Maudy explained to Mary that Elizabeth did not respect her children, including Mary, and that was a big part of her problem with handling life here. Mary's response was "You got that right," and she started to cry. The lack of respect was so bad, that according to Mary, "all we did, all the time, was argue—and argue very loud."

Then, Mary said, "What about my son, Matt? He never seems to do anything right. He's twelve years old and just doesn't listen to me. I get really annoyed with him." The mom, Ms. Elizabeth, that has passed simply delivered to Maudy the message: "He needs lots of love and respect." Mary was not especially pleased to hear this, and bristled at this message. However, as Maudy expresses to everyone, "Don't shoot the messenger...I simply deliver what I hear."

Because of Mary's upbringing, there was such a lack of respect that both Maudy and I knew she would be coming to several presentations. We were able to see her actually grow beyond this anger. It took over a year to get her to a point where she was beginning to have that self-respect for herself.

One day during the summer, she came to a presentation, and was obviously shaken. Her only son, Matt, twelve years old, had drowned in early summer. She was on the beach and could not get to him. Both Maudy and I were shocked, and we all comforted Mary. Obviously, this had changed her. We did not recognize the old angry person at all...she was a person who was broken by this life tragedy, and of course, needed that heavenly guidance.

Matt, delivered the angel whispers to Maudy: "It was not your fault that I drowned." Even though Matt was only twelve, he had fulfilled his heavenly mission here on earth, now he would be able to do earthly work from heaven.

What was obvious to Maudy and me is that now Mary understood the value of her child, and how she did not respect what she actually had in life.

Many times, people do not respect what they have in life until it is gone. Mary certainly appreciates what she had now. In fact, because of Matt, she is going to develop a foundation for children in Matt's name. She wants to help children who are in single-parent home. During this last presentation, she was formulating exactly what she wants to do with the foundation. Respect is you Ms. Mary!

Respect for Culture

At a recent presentation, we met a person who was an artist. She was of Chinese descent, and her work was becoming widely accepted. Her business had grown, so she had postponed taking a vacation for several years. Jani explained to Maudy that she did sculptures on commission. She was so enthusiastic about her accomplishments and explained how very much she loves this type of work.

Jani explained in detail that she would meet with prospective clients from all types of backgrounds and would become very interested in their cultures. She would do initial drawings and then go back to the client for their approval. Then, when all this was accomplished, she would begin the sculpture, which could take several weeks.

Further, she expressed that she did this as a type of meditation, and would throw herself totally into the sculpture. Her concern was "after she delivered the finished product to the customer, she would get sick for about one week." At first, she thought it was strange, but then realized that it was a common thing that occurred each and every time she finished a sculpture. Jani's question to Maudy: "I love what I do. Why does this happen?"

While Jani was talking to Maudy, Maudy was already getting angel whispers from Jani's grandmother. The grandmother was telling Maudy: "Jani, you are a person who has great respect for culture and people. The only thing was that when you left China as a child, you knew your culture and loved it, but you had not come back to China to renew your own sense of your culture." She agreed that this was indeed true because she moved to a new country, Belgium, and loved the culture, but put her own culture on hold. Her grandmother continued: "Once you go back to China for a visit and renew and review your own culture, all of the sickness that you felt before will be gone." Jani explained that with all the clients she truly enjoyed their stories of their own culture, but was missing her own—and yearning to go back at least one more time to visit her homeland.

Interesting how heaven works. Jani recognized that when she was respecting the cultures of others, she had neglected her own. This is why she would get sick. Finally, she gave herself permission to take a vacation to her homeland—and avoids getting sick. This is her promise to respect her culture.

Heavenly Animal Respect

Many times in presentations, animal lovers ask if animals are in heaven. Well, from my observation in all the presentations over the years with Maudy, I can tell you that they have a very special place.

For example, the anecdote earlier in this book details the time Maudy was delivering a heavenly message at an encounter and "the deer were showing their hunter where he had shot them." No blood, of course, but nevertheless, it was shown.

That particular encounter is very vivid to me and will continue to remain with me.

Sometimes, I have actually experienced Maudy delivering messages to someone who might be abusive to animals. In this case, it was clear the man was neglecting a dog. That particular person had passed, according to messages delivered through Maudy via an angel whisper was that "now he (the dog abuser) has to do earthly work from heaven, and he's doing it in animal shelters, and assisting people to find good homes for these animals."

So, do I believe that there is a special place for our furry friends? Yes, I do.

It also made it very clear to me, that animals are more important than we actually realize in the heavenly realm. After all, animals were the thought of our Creator to accompany us on this earth. Each and every creature, whether domestic or wild, has a unique purpose.

So, when we say "respect for animals," we mean it—to respect animals in all forms. Just take care of your own animals, and it doesn't hurt if you feed a stray cat or dog along the way, too.

Respect for Self in Conversation

Maudy has such a unique way of telling us things—and as she expresses it, "When it sticks, it clicks." Well, one of the things that I found so terrific and interesting when I first met Maudy is that she used the term "exchange thoughts" instead of debating or arguing. Over the years, this has become such a part of my vocabulary and way of life that I use it alongside Maudy continuously.

When you think of the phrase "exchange thoughts," it becomes very real that we can exchange thoughts and let the other person do the same, instead of standing there and screaming until you "get your ego across" and not your point. What basically happens is that the tone of voice gets louder and louder, and all that was heard was the "thunder" and nothing was accomplished. What happens is that not only did you lose respect for yourself, but the other person was not respected either.

Two weeks ago, we had a presentation, whereby a participant stated she did not want to ask a question. However, the host of the presentation encouraged her to do so and would not let her go without asking a question.

Well, then Lori asked the question: "How can I be a better mom to my fifteen-year-old son?" Then, Maudy was complimenting her on the way she was raising her four children. While she was a single mom and a professional, she was actually doing a very good job.

Then Maudy's angel whispers came through from Lori's aunt Mary Beth: "All you have to do is think and rethink before you express yourself." Lori, bristled at first, and started to get angry because she did not like this particular relative. Maudy said: "This is the relative who has permission to assist you, and she will do so in your life with your children." Maudy explained that all she had to do was "love her child in a softer way."

This is when Lori became very angry and said to Maudy: "You are wrong, I have to be strict and this is the only way he will listen. He's difficult, and yes, I raise my voice, but this is all he understands." It was obvious to me and Maudy that this conversation was not going anywhere. What she had lost was the fact that: "exchanging thoughts" is much better than screaming and raising your voice, especially with a child in their formative years. What they need is encouragement to go forward in their own demanding teenage years.

So, Maudy simply encouraged her to be "the best she can be,"and we moved to the next participant.

This was indeed the topic for the ride home. We both have gone into prayer for Lori and her family.

If we only stop and think about "exchanging thoughts" each and every time we face a difficult situation, not only will it save our sanity, it truly saves our respect and that of others.

Respect of self and others is simply one of those things that is not mysterious, just needs to be lived.

Be Kind to Your Mind
Look at what we do have
Look at what you can do
Look at who you are
Pray to God to find
The Courage to Control…your mind

On Respect: Maudisms to Remember

A Maudism (or Coat Hanger) is a phrase to memorize and hang on to when you are facing difficult situations.

> *People often neglect self respect, when they*
> *live the disease to please.*
> ....
> *Dear Lord, put your arms over my shoulders*
> *and your hand over my mouth.*
> ....
> *CCC = Control—Charge—Choice*
> ....
> *I Can and I Will*
> ....
> *When It Sticks, It Clicks*

FOUR

Patience

Patience is the gift of time. When we look at the element of patience, we must remember this will require a lot of practice. Perhaps you have had to stand in a long line at a store and you have another commitment awaiting you. Or you are in your car, anxious to get someplace, and there is a lot of traffic.

Patience is not the easiest element to live. Many people tell me the word "patience" is not in their vocabulary. Most people want to see things happen yesterday. This is when you need to realize the two most difficult days are yesterday and tomorrow. We worry about yesterday today, and we worry about tomorrow today. Then the question is where did today go?

Patience is faith. Faith is where fear will disappear. When we turn to faith, we patiently wait. All of our prayers are received, registered, documented, and reported. What this means to you is that while our prayers are being processed, you will be asked to have patience. Your prayer will be answered when the time is right.

Expecting Blessings from Heaven

When I deliver a positive message, people often ask me when it will take place. I immediately explain that I cannot say exactly what time, not even for births or deaths. We can set the clock forward and backward here on earth, but in heaven, time does not exist.

My own patience is often tested. People want to see things happen quickly and start worrying or complaining when nothing happens right away. When the whining comes to the surface, I take a deep breath and handle things in a correct and gentle manner.

When some people still don't get it and continue to complain, my tolerance level changes and I become very direct. I let this category of people, whom I refer to as the "cheese and crackers club" (so they can wine, wine, wine), kindly know that they can only see things happen when they turn to faith and patiently wait.

If Not Today, Then Maybe Tomorrow

I get very excited when I let people know what they can look forward to because I feel like it is happening to me. In the following story, I was glad that I was chosen to be a messenger because the excitement of what I had to say was so terrific.

Gail and I were invited to a private home presentation in Georgia. The turnout was very good, and among these interesting people was Candace, a forty-seven-year-old woman who came at the request of a friend.

Candace told me, in all honesty, that she was hesitant to come because of her fear of the unknown. I calmed her down and said, "It is as much a surprise for me as it is for you. I never know what I will have to say."

"Will I ever have a baby?" she asked with a smile.

Candace informed me that she had major hip surgery and had several miscarriages. She tried all the options through the medical world and was depressed, because after all, time was of the essence!

I explained to Candace that with heaven the impossible is possible. I continued, "Everything happens for a reason. It is not what happens to us, but how we handle it." I told Candace that her mother, who passed, was giving me information. The information was completely confirmed by Candace. There were elements of Candace's life, revealed by her mom, that touched her heart and she knew that it was her mother.

I looked at Candace and needed to tell her: "Congratulations! Congratulations! Congratulations!" I heard this word echo three times, so I said it three times.

"What does that mean?" she asked.

"I'm not too sure, but turn to faith and patiently wait. If not today, then maybe tomorrow." It was too overwhelming for Candace, so she stopped asking question.

I explained to the group that the mystical part about delivering messages is that I never know what will come through and actually did not know what the echo meant! Besides, I didn't want to cause some sort of shock, so to speak!

Six weeks after the original seminar, Gail received a call from a very excited Candace. She called to give the wonderful news that she was pregnant with triplets! That's what the three echoes meant! Candace sent us photocopies of the ultrasounds. The three little angels, two boys and one girl, arrived earlier this year, and all are in good health.

The patience of Candace became her happiness. Being on heaven's payroll, I am paid through her happiness, and this is my blessing.

It's Not What You Hear that Matters
It Is When You Learn to Listen

Like everyone else, I keep a very busy schedule within the house, which includes cooking and cleaning. Sometimes when I am cooking, a message is delivered to me that I know I have to relay to someone else. This is where my patience comes in, because I have to store that information until I can deliver it. The Spirit that has delivered the message is patient because in heaven there is no time and they know I will deliver the angel whispers at the appropriate earthly time.

One day, while cooking, I heard in a loud and clear voice someone saying: "Kayla's mother!" It startled me and my five cats, who were also in the kitchen. I then looked at them and said out loud: "Okay, which one of you said that?" By this time, all the cats scattered and were running off, because of the loud noise.

I was speaking to my cats to actually calm myself down and to give myself peace of mind. Even though my work is about God's miracles, keep in mind that I do not want to ever see Spirit appearances and only focus on the "listening." So, I knew in time that I would either meet this person at a presentation, or someone would call me.

Kayla's Mother

Three days later, again while cooking, my phone rang and I picked it up. I heard a lovely young voice ask: "Is this Maudy?" I said yes, and immediately asked "Are you Kayla's mother?"

There was a very long pause. I knew I had put this person in shock. It wasn't my intention to startle or frighten her, but for some unusual reason I was very excited to hear her voice. She then introduced herself as Noelle, Kayla's mother.

Then Noelle asked me: "Maudy how did you do that?" I explained that I could hear angel whispers and I tune into the frequency of people's voices. I continued that I had to tap into my patience because three days ago, her grandmother told me about her. I further explained that it was very loud and clear—that sometimes heaven does not want me to miss the call, and her grandmother was one of those people.

I explained to Noelle that her grandmother has approval from God to guide her family and those close to Kayla. Noelle then explained that she was very close to her grandmother and actually that was the reason for her call.

By this time, Grandmother was really on a roll with the angel whispers. Her grandmother was telling me that her mother has to go to the hospital for treatment. Then Noelle interrupted me saying, "Yes Maudy, my mother Doris was diagnosed with cancer and the doctors are hopeful and said she would recover." Then I continued with the message that her mother was looking forward to seeing her come home for Christmas in New York. Noelle said that she didn't have plans to go to New York and also didn't have the money. Then, I said: "Grandma said the money will be there for you and Kayla to visit Grandma…at Christmas. There is nothing more special than to celebrate Jesus' birthday with family."

Doris' call

I asked Noelle if her mother could call also give me a call, so I could deliver more messages from her grandmother and she called the next day.

Doris, Noelle's Mom, called and we had a wonderful conversation. During the conversation she expressed her living with fear of the unknown. Doris was very clear and gave beautiful messages to soothe her daughter here on earth. It is my mission to release the fear and enlighten her life to remove that heavy mental luggage. Our conversation and three subsequent conversations were all about peace and love. She thanked me and told me that she had a tremendous sense of peace in her life.

Home for Christmas

Noelle then called me to let me know that she received an unexpected check from the insurance company. She was so happy with this money that she decided to go and be with her mother. She had a wonderful time with her mother, and Kayla was so excited to see her grandmother. They exchanged stories of what "Grandmother" had told them through angel whispers and found great solace in these stories.

Sadly, three days after Christmas, Noelle's mother, Doris passed away. After the funeral, Noelle called me and asked, "Maudy, did you know my mother was going to pass?" I answered, "No, I didn't, I only had instructions to bring you all together. It is my mission to relieve hardship, and provide chances and choices."

Angel Wings

Noelle got in touch with me forty days after Doris passed. She asked me if her mother was okay and if she had messages for her. I told her that her mother Doris arrived in God's Kingdom and her family welcomed her in heaven. I also told her that her mother had beautiful news for her.

The next thing that happened to me was extraordinary; it was "out of this world." Heaven showed me the most beautiful scenario all within less than thirty seconds.

I told Noelle that I could "see" heaven's door, more like a gate, open up with a bright light shining through. At the same time, a beautiful angel came out of the gate and Doris was going into this door/gate and embracing this beautiful angel. Then the angel changed into a beautiful little girl, giving her wings to Doris. The wings were feathery and had indescribably gorgeous colors. I felt privileged to witness this; it was a true glimpse behind the scenes of heaven. I had never ever experienced this heavenly sight while working for heaven. It gave me the familiar goosebumps and chills, which in the spiritual world is acknowledgment from heaven.

Wonderful News

Noelle started to cry and said: "Maudy, after meeting and experiencing you, I know that I have recognized that I will spend my heaven doing good here on earth. I have also learned to 'see' and to 'listen' to all God wants me to recognize and confirm. I also had to be patient for those forty days to talk after my mom passed, because I had so many questions, and you know that wasn't easy for me. Also, Maudy I am pregnant, and hope the baby is born on my mother's birthday!"

I explained to Noelle that her mother was "called home to heaven" so she could guide this beautiful angel child throughout her life here on earth. The baby, a girl, was born a day before her mother's birthday—on my…birthday! How cool is that? Again, being on God's payroll for me is wonderful—and it was my blessed "payday."

Prayers and Meditations Build Patience

It wasn't easy for Noelle. Not only did she have to have patience with the situation at hand, her mother in New York having cancer while she lived far away; but then, her mother passed away. And then she got pregnant. All of this requires a lot of patience and through prayer and meditations she will continue to do well.

Again, in life it is not how long you live, but how you live. No matter how life throws us a curveball or how it can ambush us, try to look at the moral and why you had to endure this. Remember it's not what happens to you, but how you handle what happens to you.

Let prayers and meditation lead you, because this is how you will build patience. The process of learning is not only to memorize the psalms or scripture—the focus is how to live it over 100 percent in Faith and the rest will come—and you will build and create that patience that will become YOU!

We can always count on God … but can He count on us?

When Life Throws You a Curveball

What do we usually do when unexpected things happen in our lives? We scream, cry, yell, and perhaps even panic. Sometimes you do not have time to do any of these things because, let's face it, life happens. This is when you need to put patience into practice.

The following story is just one of those happenings that shows how heaven works in rather mysterious ways.

On November 10, 2004, Gail and I made our first trip to Holland to meet with a potential book publisher. Our first stop in Holland was in Odoorn, in the province of Drenthe. We drove almost three hours to reach our destination of De Oringer Marke Hotel, which was nestled in a storybook surrounding. It was quite beautiful. We were very tired, so we parked our car and literally dragged our suitcases and ourselves up a long and narrow path to the hotel.

The desk clerk greeted us and we asked if we could share a room. He said, "Oh no, we have two separate rooms for you. This is what was arranged." We asked if our rooms were close to each other, as we like to compare the happenings of the day. He assured us we were next door to each other.

We took the elevator to the second floor and thought it best to take a nap before we met with the publishing staff that evening. We slept for about three hours and then met the publisher and staff for dinner. We stayed with them until about 10:30 p.m., when we returned to the hotel.

Still in a state of excitement, Gail and I spent another thirty minutes in her room going over our very busy day. Then it was time to get some real rest, and I went back to my room. I was very exhausted and immediately fell asleep.

Around midnight, I woke up with an incredible start. There was an alarm blaring! Gail called me and said, "What is that?"

"Gail, it's a fire. Get dressed and pack your suitcase now!" We both went into the hallway and looked at each other. We didn't smell any smoke and noticed that no one came out of any of the rooms. We were curious if other guests were packing and getting ready to leave their rooms. We were both amazed that no one came out of a room because of this ear-splitting alarm! How could anyone still be sleeping?

I went in Gail's room, and we could hardly hear ourselves speak. I said, "Gail, did the alarm push your door open?" In Holland, the hotel doors will not lock unless the key is left in the door on the inside.

"No. Was your door open?"

"Yes. I thought that the alarm had pushed my door open. The key was still in my door!"

The alarm went on for a good five to seven minutes, with no sight or smell of smoke or fire, and no one had come out of their rooms or to ours to warn us of what was happening. I thought that we must be alone in this hotel and would have to move.

Finally, after what seemed like an eternity, the alarm stopped. There was still no one in the hallway to see if anyone else was getting up or was even concerned. I was, however, concerned about my door being open when the alarm went off.

Gail said, "Why don't you come and sleep in my room?"

"No, I'll be okay."

"Okay, if you change your mind, let me know."

About twenty minutes later, I decided to call Gail and take her up on being roommates. At this time, I asked Gail if anything unusual had happened in her room. She said no. I proceeded to tell her that I heard two spirits in my room. I did not want to open my eyes, but I knew they were there because they made their presence known.

One spirit was an older woman, possibly a mom or a grandmother, and the other was a child with a rag doll. I could feel the doll hitting me. It was as if a small child was playing with a toy and not paying attention to anyone around her. I knew that one of the spirits was named Greta. I could hear feet rustling back and forth in my room and feel someone sitting on my bed. Gail said, "Well, nothing like that happened in here," and asked if we should leave the light on. I said I didn't care. We left the light on in our bedroom to sleep for the remainder of that night and the next. We didn't want any more visitors!

The next morning, Gail and I had made the decision to room together in her room! She was very concerned about me going in my room alone and asked if she could help get my items. I insisted that I wanted to go into this room alone to pray for these people and get my things.

On our way down to breakfast that morning, I noticed the chambermaids were cleaning the other rooms on our floor. There were obviously people in those rooms, because chambermaids only clean rooms that have been occupied. But no one had come out of their rooms the evening before in response to the alarm. I asked the hotel clerk how many guests were registered the evening before. He replied, "Six other guests. It is winter and people do not vacation a lot this time of year in Holland. It's cold."

After breakfast, we decided to go for a walk. We were scheduled to have lunch with the publisher and wanted to enjoy the area for the rest of the morning. Gail ventured out ahead of me with her camera to get a few extra shots of this quaint hotel and surrounding village. She remarked it looked like a "Hansel and Gretel" village and she wanted to capture as much as she could on film.

She walked down that same long and narrow path that we had dragged our suitcases up the previous day. There was something in the distance that looked like statues, and I wasn't sure what it was. Then, I could see Gail had stopped in front of them, and was taking pictures.

Suddenly she paused, and she called out to me: "Maudy, my goodness, please come here and look at this!" So, I caught up with her and we both stood in front of these two very impressive bronze life-sized statues of an adult woman and a child in traditional Holland dress. Gail said, "I think these individuals might be related to the unexpected visitors last evening. Oh my, look at this child. She has something in her hand."

We both got goosebumps when we realized that the little girl statue held a doll. I realized that these were indeed the two spirits that visited me. Both of us looked at these bronze figures in sheer amazement!

After the initial shock of this, we went inside and waited to meet the publisher. We told the publisher what had happened the night before, and he said he knew there had been a fire in the hotel during the 1800s and the people commemorated in the statues perished in a fire on that site. We asked that he and his staff pray for these individuals, as it was necessary for them to go to their eternal resting place. We came to the conclusion that due to the fire, which took both of their lives, for some reason, they didn't go forward. This happens many times in tragic deaths or if people do not pray for these souls.

After an exhausting trans-Atlantic flight, Gail and I did not expect to have visitors. Did life throw us a curveball? You bet! However, with some patience and prayer, we were able to help these souls go forward and continue the work that we were sent to Holland to complete.

The Seven Strangers on the Continued Journey

Our unexpected visitors in Odoorn certainly left a lasting impression. However, we didn't realize it at the time, but the best was truly yet to come on this rather interesting journey.

Prior to going to Holland, I had renewed my Dutch passport, and I had other American identification with me, such as my American driver's license and my social security card. Everything seemed in order. Gail was really excited because this was her first trip to Europe.

Our trip was mostly business, though we'd have an opportunity to visit friends and relatives. We started our trip in Odoorn and continued our journey. Besides meeting with the publisher, this trip was our way of marketing, and we planned to visit various media outlets.

We went to a local television station to see a high official. This man made it clear that we had only twenty minutes to present ourselves (though we were delighted just to get our foot in the door). He grilled Gail with the usual questions: Was she my agent? What was her purpose? She explained that we are a team and work together to bring people to peace. She further explained that I am a mystic messenger and that I use my gift to assist people along life's journey.

The questioning went on for some time. We pointed out that there is teaching involved throughout our presentations. Then he started to ask me questions. Now I was able to get to the business of angels. I related various things to him that only he could identify. His folded arms and standoffish stance was obviously a shield of defense. He was apprehensive until some of his questions were answered. A person named Ben, who had passed on, was a dear friend who had incredible words of encouragement and enlightenment to pass along. His eyes started to fill with tears, and I knew that he was aware that the conversation and message delivered was the real deal. During the conversation, he even sent away a very persistent associate who wanted his immediate attention. He told her that he would tend to this situation in a little while.

Twenty minutes turned into almost two hours. This man didn't want to leave our sides. He walked us to the elevator and continued to talk. He then embraced us both as newfound friends.

We booked a hotel close to the airport and were getting anxious to head back home. We missed our families and we were running low on money. However, we managed to get a few inexpensive souvenirs from the hotel gift shop for our families.

Since Gail and I both paint, I noticed a Rembrandt figurine and thought it would be a nice souvenir from Holland. She said, "I've never seen a real Rembrandt, I guess I should have a remembrance of him. After all, I made a trip to his country!"

The day of departure, we got up early to pack, eat breakfast, and get to the airport for the 7 a.m. check-in time. We turned in our car and breathed a sigh of relief. Homeward bound! We made it through customs and pushed our big suitcases, three each, up to the ticket counter. Gail was first in line and everything went okay. I was next, but after a few moments, the agent said, "I'm sorry, you cannot leave Holland. You don't have the appropriate paperwork." Needless to say, both of our mouths fell open.

Our questions were rattled off in rapid succession: What did we need? Could we get on the next flight? What paperwork did we need to leave the country? The answer I received was that I needed a letter of transportation to leave the country and another letter to be admitted back into the United States. I also needed a copy of my resident alien card, which was in Charlotte, North Carolina.

The airline person stated that we could possibly make the 11:30 a.m. flight. It was now 7:30 a.m. We went to get the rental car that we had just turned in and go back to the airport hotel and ask if we could leave our baggage there, as we didn't know if we would be able to leave the same day.

The next few hours were nerve-racking but totally exhilarating. We took a bus, then a train, then a tram, and finally a walk to the American embassy. We knew that we were on the right track when we met two young women, Lena and Rosa, on the train who directed us to the embassy. Both women were from Russia, married to men from Holland, and trying to get visas to go home for a visit to Russia. Luckily, they spoke fluent Dutch and I was able to communicate with them.

We arrived at the embassy and got in line around 10 a.m. We knew we would not be able to make the next flight out of Holland. We met three young men while we were in line. They were also seeking visas to go to the United States. One was a native Dutchman who was going to attend college in the Midwest, and another was from China and heading to Pennsylvania for college. The third man was from Turkey and was going to New York City to be with relatives. He also planned to attend college while he was visiting. Our conversations with them were terrific.

They had never been to America and were interested in everything American. The hour of standing in the cold really went by quickly. I passed along messages to each young man.

When we got to the gate around 11 a.m., a guard told us we'd have to come back between 2 and 4 p.m. because it was a question of not having my registered alien card. Even though we were disappointed and cold, we thought we'd walk to a nearby café and have lunch. To our amazement, the Rijks Museum, home to many original Rembrandt paintings, was behind us.

While ordering lunch, we noticed two faces peering in the restaurant window from the outside. It was Lena and Rosa. Lena joined us for lunch and Rosa stayed only for a few moments and said she'd be back later. I had messages for both, but particularly for Lena. She was an only child and had lost both her parents. She wanted to go back to Russia to see a few distant relatives. Lena's mother had many loving and beautiful messages for her, and there were a lot of tears of joy. It was an affirmation that was necessary for Lena to comfort her soul.

Because we had extra time, we managed to visit the Rijks Museum, which had some of the most beautiful paintings we had ever seen. The Rembrandt figurine we purchased the night before suddenly became lifelike for both me and

Gail. It is what I refer to as a preview of life. Did I know that we were going there? No, but obviously heaven did.

We walked back to the embassy and got in line again. Finally, after two checkpoints, we got up to the window. Mr. Gronian told me I could not leave the country without a copy of my alien card, and there would be a fine. The first item on the list of things to do was to have pictures taken at a local passport area and bring them back to the embassy so a letter of transportation could be drawn up. However, Mr. Gronian made no promises.

We found out that the embassy would be closing soon, so time was of the essence. We rushed out, found a photography place, and headed back to the embassy to give the photos to Mr. Gronian. We got his direct phone number and a fax number so I could ask Micheal, my husband, to fax the information. Mr. Gronian, again, made no promises and advised us to cancel our flight until further notice. This is not exactly what you want to hear when you are trying to leave the country and go home.

We took the same tram, train, and bus back to the airport hotel and asked if we could stay the night. Thankfully they had a room available. It was late by this time, so we headed to the Italian restaurant in the hotel.

We were encouraging each other and knew that all would be well. All of a sudden, Gail said, "Look, Maudy." In the middle of the restaurant was a statue of Mary, holding the baby Jesus, with a candle in front of it. During our entire ten-day stay in the Netherlands, we did not see one religious icon displayed anyplace. I wasn't even able to get into the church where I worshipped as a child. The church was closed because of a lack of priests.

This sculpture of Mary and Jesus was out of character with everything else we had seen during our trip, so it really took us both by surprise. I knew once I saw this holy reminder that we would be fine. I asked the waiter if he could light the candle, and he did. A prayer was offered and we sat down to our meal.

Meanwhile, my husband got up in the middle of the night to fax a copy of my alien card to Mr. Gronian at the embassy. We went to bed a little lighthearted that evening but still in full prayer. We learned in this situation that it is not what happens to you but how you handle it.

The next morning we made our trek to the embassy. We met Edith, who was from Indonesia, and her British husband, while we were in line. Edith was very friendly and mentioned the sadness of her mom's passing three months ago. She was embarking on a new life with her husband and heading to Florida. Her mom was already giving me a message and said, "Thank you for taking care of me, now live your life." Edith became very emotional and hugged me.

When we got to Mr. Gronian, he still had not received the information from my husband and asked us to come back at 4 p.m. Here we were again in Amsterdam with free time. This must have been the universe's way of allowing us to sightsee. We walked around a few streets, and Gail took great pictures of the markets and canals. We decided to go back to the café in front of the Rijks Museum for a late lunch.

While at this café, we met a woman from South Carolina, who had accompanied her husband on a business trip. She was alone and decided to join us for lunch. Many messages were delivered to her from her family. She was somewhat surprised but very pleased.

Finally, we headed back to the embassy and breathed a huge sigh of relief. Mr. Gronian had all the paperwork in order. We could pay the fine and catch an airplane the following morning.

We finally arrived in Atlanta, Georgia, our port of entry in the United States, and encountered more checkpoints. Then we were called aside and had to go into a separate room to meet with officials. This was more than a little unnerving at this point in time. After about ten minutes, all papers were accepted and we were allowed to continue our trip home to Charlotte.

Once we were safely on American soil and on our way to Charlotte, Gail said to me, "I firmly believe you are a mystic because if you were a psychic, we certainly would not have been in this situation!"

We were only detained for two days, but during that time we met seven different people from seven different cultures. I am convinced all of these individuals were placed on our path by a higher authority. Nothing in life is ever a coincidence. Not only were these people interesting, but I was delighted to assist them on their life's journey.

Our experience was an extreme test of our patience, but in the end, everything worked according to plan. When you live in the moment you need to follow through on all aspects being presented to you. This is what Gail and I did. We didn't give up and there was not a discouraging word exchanged. Just one day at a time, and in this case, it was one hour at a time.

All Will Be Well
Embrace the good, reject the bad
Prevent yourself from being sad
Keep the peace, Teach the peace
Live at ease
Don't be stressed or depressed
It's not what happens to you
It's how you handle what happens to you
It's all going to be fine in time
Life is Love
And All Will Be Well

On Patience: Maudisms to Remember

A Maudism (or Coat Hanger) is a phrase to memorize and hang on to when you are facing difficult situations.

> *Patience is the gift of time*
> ....
> *When we turn to Faith, we patiently wait*
> ....
> *If not today, then maybe tomorrow*
> ....
> *It's not what you hear that matters,*
> *   it is when you learn to listen*
> ....
> *It's not what happens to you, but how*
> *   you handle what happens to you*
> ....
> *The process of learning life is how to live it*
> ....
> *Put patience into practice*
> ....
> *Live in the moment, whatever you do,*
> *   follow through.*

FIVE

Courage

Courage is the fifth element of the spiritual law, and it takes our willpower to open up this door. Courage is strength. Look at your strength and never your weakness. Once you open the door to courage, your life changes completely. You will see miracles happen.

The lack of courage can block us from many things in life and create a chain of negative reactions, such as fear, uncertainty, and unhappiness. All of these emotions can block you from making important decisions.

When people are in a depressed state, the cause usually stems from a lack of courage to make the changes within themselves. People will often say, "Maudy, I don't know why I can't get out of this situation. How do I find the courage?" I respond by asking, "Do you want to find courage and make changes with yourself?" Then, I explain the serenity prayer: "God grant us the serenity to accept the things we cannot change, the courage to change the things we can, and the wisdom to know the difference."

Courage is the element that you will need to restructure self-love and self-respect. Once you do this, you will notice that stress, frustration, and depression will disappear. When we tap into courage, all of the negative energy will disappear. You will notice that when you open your door to courage, many of the other doors will open themselves for you.

The Willpower to Climb Every Mountain

We are here not to change the world or other people, but to find the courage to change the things we can, which starts with ourselves! It takes self-realization to recognize the habits and life patterns that need to change. Doing so will let life work with you and not against you. We have the wisdom to see the difference in life challenges if we open the door of courage. We are able to climb and even move mountains!

Marie-Anna was searching for her parental grandmother. No one in the family knew anything about her, including her name or what she looked like. The search was very real for Marie-Anna. It was a part of her heritage and she wanted to find a connection.

Marie-Anna had attended two presentations and each time, one of her relatives told her to take a trip to her homeland of Haiti. She was very clear that she did not want to go because of the turmoil in the country. I informed Marie-Anna at presentation number three to go to Haiti. This was a very firm message that many of her questions and longings of home would be answered once she took this trip.

Marie-Anna had lived in the United States for nineteen years and had never gone back to Haiti because of the political unrest. It was going to take a lot of courage for her to make the trip. She knew from relatives that this beautiful paradise had been destroyed and would not be what she remembered as a child. Finally, she decided that now was the time to follow through on her instructions from above. She had found the courage and went for a two-week vacation.

Marie-Anna went to the places that her ancestors mentioned by name. One was a beautiful church that was part of her pilgrimage. I mentioned on two occasions to go to La Croix (the cross) in Haiti. Marie-Anna was in awe that I knew about the place and could even pronounce it correctly. She followed her instructions but wasn't sure why she needed to do this. But since she was in the area, she thought, why not?

La Croix was located in a beautiful village on top of a mountain on the northwestern side of Haiti. With reluctance, she decided to climb the mountain. The only other transportation was motorcycle, donkey, or a small bus, which didn't look safe. Climbing seemed the only safe option.

An older woman stood beside her and said she'd like to come with her. There had been no one there earlier, and this woman just seemed to appear out of nowhere. Marie-Anna thought to herself that it would be nice to have company, since she wasn't sure how long the trek up the mountain would take. The women spoke about many things, particularly their ancestors, during this two-hour trip to the top of the mountain. Marie-Anna thought it was a bit strange that the woman, Louise, kept calling her "my child."

A very strong and unique bond was being created, and Marie-Anna kept wondering about this woman and her grandmotherly way of approaching life. When the women said their goodbyes, Marie-Anna continued on her trip and went to visit one of her cousins in a nearby town. The cousin said that some of the ancestors on her father's side might be from that area of La Croix. Marie-Anna was surprised and told her cousin about Louise.

Upon her return to the United States, Marie-Anna decided to come to another presentation. I asked, "Who was the person that climbed the mountain with you?"

"Oh, it was just a woman," she said, a little flustered.

"During the conversation, did she call you 'my child'?"

"Yes, that's correct."

"Because you are! It was your grandmother in spirit who was working through Louise, who accompanied you to that mountaintop."

Because of Marie-Anna's extreme courage, other things were revealed about her grandmother. I was told that she came from the ships as a released slave from one of the islands. Jamaica was a stop for the ships, but not necessarily her home island. I also heard "Guinea-Bissau" and something about Africa and Kenya.

She was also from a tribe that was described as the Mandinka tribe. This tribe, according to the angels' information, kept very much to itself and traveled a lot. I described the woman as having a round face and very large, expressive, happy eyes. Marie-Anna was going to research this tribe because now she could find out something about the long-lost family history. She later e-mailed us to say she was tracking all this fascinating information and all of the information was filling the pieces of history that she longed to know all because of angel whispers.

Marie-Anna's extreme courage to go into a war-torn country was rewarded. Not only was she safe and protected but she actually had the honor to be accompanied by her actual ancestor in spirit.

Loss Prevention

The loss prevention I refer to is how to save the valuable part of your life: you. Gail and I encounter many people from all walks of life at our presentations. In my world of outreach, I am also challenged. I often mention that I am not here to prove me. I am here to prove you.

Recognizing stubbornness is both interesting and funny. First of all, I know that some people in attendance will deny their own family in heaven or earth, and their second questions are usually based on denying my answers.

When speaking with a woman named Patricia at a presentation, I kept asking, "Who is Margaret? Who is John?" With arms folded, she said, "I don't know." For me, the messages were getting louder. I said again, "Are you sure you don't know anyone with that name?"

She then said, "Oh well, Margaret is the name of my mother, and my father's name is John." Everyone in attendance looked at Patricia with awe. Gail and I—and the others in attendance—are always amazed at this stubbornness. Of course, we were also amused that the woman wasn't able to readily identify her parents!

You might ask that if I know this already, why would I continue? The answer is pretty simple. My clarity of mind is to be the conscience of their mind, and since this type of person wants to challenge me, I have to challenge them right back.

These people are usually lost in their own world and are uncertain if they want answers. I have to simply handle the conversation with love and kindness in order for them to have clarity.

Ann's Story

Ann came to a presentation and asked a question about her job: Should she stay or should she go?

I heard the name Jan and asked Ann "Who is Jan or Janet?" Of course, she didn't know anyone from her past or the present by that name. I continued to give her choices and directions, but her attitude showed she had no interest. My clarity of mind was to recognize that she had a problem with the solution of job opportunities. This may sound crazy, but I was aware that she simply wasn't ready for change or any solutions that might come her way.

Ann could not focus because she was in conflict with someone. The person she was in conflict with was actually Jan, her sister-in-law. Since I was aware of this, I asked her to say the name of the person she has problems with and she answered, "Oh, her name is Janet." The people at the presentation sighed and I just smiled.

I told her that in time everything would be okay and moved on to the next person to assist. I need to maintain my clarity and will not allow a stubborn person to drain me or cause unnecessary aggravation for the people at the presentation who are anxious to move on. Some people are happy being unhappy and prefer to remain in the lost rather than the found department.

When Can I Be with Mom?

The following story is about Molly, who asked the question, "When can I be with Mom?" It seems like a logical question until you realize that Mom has passed! Molly's mom was eighty-two years old when she died, and Molly had been her mother's caregiver.

Molly was very unhappy and experienced depression as a result of her mom's passing and the difficult family situations that presented themselves after the funeral.

Heavenly messages are always right on track and right on time. Ruth, Molly's mom, introduced herself to me and delivered a message about a cross-stitch hanging on Molly's wall. I asked Molly, "Did your mom cross-stitch the serenity prayer that hangs on a wall in your home?" Molly broke down and started sobbing, and soon the entire room was in tears.

Since Ruth was so loud and clear, I wanted her to go home with Molly and not with me. Therefore, it was necessary for me to give Molly a hug to console her. This is also the way those that have passed give hugs to those here on earth. People in heaven do not have the same levels of emotion as we do. They only experience love.

I told Molly I would see her again and we'd continue with this conversation. Sure enough, about six months later, I saw a beautiful young woman come into a presentation. Molly told me she was able to assist her brother with his problems, had gotten over her anger, and was indeed taking one day at a time. She knew the serenity prayer and said that prayer and the angel whispers helped her get her life back together. This is how heaven pays me. This woman was now on the right track and able to go forward and help others. This is how you pay it forward.

The Energy of Your Mind

Our mind has a powerful energy. It can make us or break us. It takes courage to recognize that the energy that you have in your own mind is real. Sometimes people feel they might just be thinking about something, but really it is your mind processing the energy that you need to go forward in life. In other words, hurtful things go without thinking and heartfelt things require thinking. It takes courage to do and say the right thing.

Everything starts in the presence of your mind. Remember the phrases, "Happiness is a state of mind" or "I am losing my mind"? We all have a choice, and prayer and meditation are two choices that will help us maintain a healthy, happy mind. We need to make time for ourselves to enjoy life.

Create Your Own Positive Journal

Once you recognize your energy, you can transmit it to writing. This is where journaling comes in. It takes courage to recognize those feelings, and writing them down soothes your inner emotions so you can start healing.

Keep your thoughts positive, do positive things, stay positive, and be around positive people. Gail has suggested keeping a "Thirty-Day Positive Journal" and write down one thing per day that is positive. Regardless of the day's events, you can find at least one positive aspect per day to enter into this journal. I think this is a terrific way to form a new habit and practice the power of positive thinking. By completing this practice, you will be able to have clarity of mind and be alert at all times.

Read powerful, positive self-help books and articles to increase your self-realization, self-awareness, and self-confidence. Remind yourself that life is what we allow and who we allow. Make the world a better place—but start with yourself first. Then, you can help others and look forward to life's surprises.

Every Life Story Has a Moral

In the inspirational educational part of each presentation, Gail and I often answer and clarify the "why" questions that people present to us. We explain why people endure hardship on their life's journey. To clarify the concept, every life story has a moral. However, we usually don't see or understand what we need to learn while a particular scenario unfolds. We mentioned in the previous chapters that we are here for our own purpose, goal, and destiny. When our emotions are in the way, they block us from understanding our life situation and we end up with familiar headache or heartache.

For me, it is very clear to recognize the moral of the life story from people revealing their particular hardship, which can result in a learning curve for them.

The Moral of My Story

Because I am gifted, life can become rather tricky, but is always very interesting for me. Let me share the moral of my own story with you.

I usually get the familiar goosebumps from when I share heavenly news. However, when it happens to me, I become speechless and feel freezing cold. I became an American citizen in December 2008. Within thirty days I received a summons in the mail for jury duty, and I was looking forward to this experience.

I told my mother-in-law that I was excited to be called for jury duty. She said, "Maudy, you can't do this." I said, "Why? I am legal. I am a citizen."

My mother-in-law was laughing and said, "Maudy, you have a gift, and if you are selected for a criminal case, it can work against you in the future. The lawyer will prosecute you if you don't inform the court now. You have to let them know about your gift."

Gail wrote a letter to the court system and advised me to give it to the judge so I could be excused from jury duty. She explained how it could be detrimental to the judicial system for all parties concerned because I am gifted. I brought the letter to the courthouse and immediately presented it to the official. He said, "When you are selected, please give this to the judge and he will make the decision."

I sat down with about a hundred other people awaiting possible selection. I thought this could be an all-day thing, and it was. The first thirty-five people were chosen for a civil case, then another twenty-five were selected.

While we were waiting, I watched a movie entitled, *The Ultimate Gift*. It was about a young man whose wealthy father passed away. This young man loved to party and enjoyed the life of being rich. He lost his money because of poor choices. His father did not leave him anything after his passing, but his father left a video where he stated he had to work for his inheritance and encouraged his son to understand intangible gifts. He also had to learn to recognize people who have been put on his path and evaluate each person to figure out why this person was there and what message was being presented to him. At first, this young man wanted to walk away and put up a wall around himself—resisting everything that came his way.

The man then met a young girl about eleven years old who had leukemia, and she taught him to look at life differently. At the end of the movie, the little girl died and the man married her mother. He then received a big check from his father's inheritance and put it to good use by building a children's hospice in the girl's name.

It was very interesting that this movie was about the intangible gifts. Since I hardly ever watch movies, it seemed quite obvious how heaven was showing me a familiar scenario. I was captivated by how this movie was so much about what Gail and I present to the public in our teaching world. I felt it was talking directly to me.

What took me by surprise was that the movie was filmed in Charlotte, North Carolina, where Gail and I live. I knew that this was heaven giving me the message because this story also showed sacrifice and the intangible gifts that lead to his inheritance. He felt purpose driven in building this hospital. I recognized many similar aspects in this scenario and my message became very clear.

After the movie ended, there were twenty-five more people selected for a criminal case, and my name was again not announced. I talked to people who were picked for jury duty and they said they had to attend the whole week. When it was close to five o'clock in the evening, the court officials told us we could go home. It was a long day, since I had been there from 8 a.m.

I thought to myself, "Great, I am off the hook!" I was relieved I didn't have to use the letter that Gail had written. It would have presented a difficult situation for the judge and me.

I went outside and was waiting for my husband to pick me up when a young lady I had briefly spoken to in the morning came up to me and asked if I had children.

I answered her and said, "Yes, two daughters." She then said, "They will be protected when you go on your journey!" She smiled and said, "Oh, there's my ride. Bye!" I now felt goosebumps for me.

I walked up to another lady who was waiting for her husband and asked if she was picked for jury duty and she said no. I told her my story and that I was glad I wasn't selected because of my gift. She smiled and didn't say anything, I thought I'd better explain and asked her if she had heard about angel whispers, mystics, or saints. She grabbed her purse and said, "I have something for you," and gave me a magazine about mystics and saints. I thanked her and gave her my book in exchange. Again she smiled and then said, "Oh, I have to go, my dear, there is my ride!"

I recognized why I had to go to court and why I wasn't selected. I didn't come for jury duty. I had to come for me. After reviewing the scenarios and the experience of the jury duty process, I learned and realized I had to watch this movie to understand and recognize my moral of life, in life, and for life. I had to meet these people who each had a message for me. I had to learn to see how God's plan is unfolding to fulfill my own mission.

The Moral of Our Trip

To show you how heaven works to protect us I will share the story of when Gail and I went to the Netherlands on November 13, 2008, for business.

We arrived at the Charlotte airport and it was misting a bit. Our flight appeared to be on time, which is nice when you have an international connecting flight! The flight attendants were very busy changing the flight boards and our plane was delayed one hour. At this point, we were not too concerned because we had plenty of time to make our evening flight in Newark, New Jersey. The flight times kept changing. Finally, after more than two hours of delay, we were allowed to board the plane only to hear the pilot announce that we still did not have clearance from the air-traffic controllers. So we sat another two hours on the tarmac before we were allowed to leave.

When we got into Newark, New Jersey, it was about fifteen minutes before our international flight to Amsterdam and everyone was in line to change their flights. So, Gail and I got up to the desk to check the status of our flight because we couldn't find it on the board.

The airline reservation clerk said, "Oh, I am sorry. Your flight for Amsterdam left ten minutes ago and I've booked you for a flight at seven tomorrow morning." Gail asked if she could book us on a flight that night since we had a presentation in Amsterdam. The clerk answered, "Yes, I can put you on a flight to Paris, France, and then to Amsterdam. It leaves in ninety minutes." We accepted and went to our next post. This flight was delayed by thirty minutes due to earlier flight groundings in Newark. We were certainly tested on our patience.

We arrived in Paris midmorning and the pilot announced we'd have to go to a reservations clerk at the airport to check connections. As we were disembarking from the aircraft, Gail looked around and remarked, "Maudy, something doesn't look right here. There are a lot of television cameras and crews everywhere." We weren't sure what was going on but followed the pilot's instructions and went to a clerk. This is when we were notified that the pilots of Air France were on strike.

The reservations clerk gave us a tentative ticket for a flight to Amsterdam on Air France. By this time, Gail and I had planned to drive to Amsterdam if the flights were not going to leave that day. We did not allow this obstacle to panic us in any way. We worked with what was in front of us. I was ready to step into my courage.

When we arrived at the gate, you guessed it, we had to wait again. This delay was only for two hours, and it was apparently the last flight out of Paris.

We finally arrived at Schipol/Amsterdam airport at about 3 p.m., hours after our intended arrival time. When we got to the baggage carousel in Amsterdam our bags were not there! We reported to the lost luggage personnel and were each given a black bag that contained a pair of socks, a T-shirt, toothpaste, a hairbrush, and few other necessities. This certainly is a very good example of how to work with what is in front of you.

I tapped into my gift and knew that the suitcases were there, but no one wanted to look any further so we headed to our hotel. Once we got to our room—after hiking up six floors of stairs (no elevator)—it was 7:30 in the evening, twelve hours from our initial time of arrival.

The next morning, we had brunch around 11:30 a.m., and still no suitcases. We had a driver picking us up around 2:30 p.m. to take us to our presentation, so we knew we had a little time and we were still practicing our patience. While eating, we were notified by the front desk that the airline had delivered our suitcases. Our patience had paid off! We arrived at our presentation, a bit tired, but with fresh clothes and ready to face about six hundred people.

The night before we were scheduled to leave, we were notified by phone that our book *Heavenly Messages* was chosen by *ParaVisie Magazine* as the best international inspirational book of 2008. The other nominees in the category were Deepak Chopra and Dr. Wayne Dyer. We were very surprised and it was a blessing to our trip.

The moral of these stories is that when we have faith, we are taken care of, and all will be well. Sometimes we need to sit back and review what has happened to us and why. What is the moral of your story? Sit back and reflect. What would you have changed? Could you have changed it? Or did it happen in order to help you to move forward and allow others to learn the moral of their own story?

Time Is a Gift

Minal is an eighty-one-year-old woman from India. Her daughter Kyra asked me to talk to her mother while she was visiting. Minal said to me, "I've heard so much about you, but I was hesitant to speak to you because I am very negative and depressed. Now I am afraid and can hardly sleep because it is like something inside of me that told me to talk to you." She then told me she was being admitted to the hospital later that week to have a tumor in her throat removed.

I told her, "Minal, you have wasted so many years and so much time by being sad. Now is the time to make right what you have to make right. You are such a beautiful lady inside and out and the only one who doesn't know it is you. You have rejected people, family, and friends, and for what?" She interrupted me and said, "Maudy, but you don't know how hard my life was and I'm always sick and nobody understands me!"

The lady on the other line in heaven was touching base with her past. I knew I had to be careful with Minal because I knew she had never looked inside herself and I did not want it to be too much of a shock. However, she was placed on my path to give her a chance and a choice to make changes. All we have to do is get the message across.

I asked Minal, "Who is Nora?" She replied, "She is my aunt who died long time ago. I never liked her and she never liked me either!" She continued, "Aunt Nora was real mean and negative. Of all people, why did Aunt Nora have to come?" I explained to her that I never know who will have approval from heaven to come and give a message.

Then I asked her, "What does 'puney' and 'manak' mean?"

Kyra joined the conversation and explained that *puney* in Hindi meant "good deeds" and *manak* was "dad." Minal was very emotional at this time and asked me how I knew this and said I spoke good Hindi. I immediately said, "No sorry, I'm Dutch. The lady in heaven told me this. Isn't that cool?" But she was still pretty upset about her aunt coming to visit.

I then told her that her dad, who was the manak, joined the conversation and wanted her to know that he loves her. I continued saying that puney in her language means good deeds, and that's exactly what heaven wants her to do.

I explained to Minal, "Aunt Nora chose you because you are so much like her. Now you need to forgive her and forgive yourself. This aunt has the mission to help someone who was as negative as she was so she chose you. You have to touch base with love because love is the key and password for you to move forward."

She asked about puney and good deeds, and I explained to her that tonight before she goes to bed, she needs to say, "I love myself and honor and respect myself." She needs to say the same thing in the morning and then call one of her children or grandchildren and tell them she loves them—but nothing more. I told her, "Also, you are to call a friend from the past who you haven't talked to for quite some time and ask how they are doing. When they are asking about you and say how you are doing, your answer will be 'I am just fine!'"

Minal told me, "Maudy, you give me homework that is simple, but yet so difficult!"

I said, "Because love is simplicity, the difficult part is can you have love and forgiveness for you and your aunt Nora?"

Then she asked me, "Where am I going when I die? I am so scared. Will heaven forgive me for being so negative all my life?"

I smiled and said, "Minal, now is the time to turn to faith, therefore fear will disappear. You will be forgiven. You need to forgive yourself and go into prayer. Please stick with your heavenly instructions. It is how we do good here on earth."

I prayed for Minal the day she went to the hospital. I received a phone call from her daughter Kyra later that afternoon. She was very excited and put her mother on the phone. With her hoarse voice, Minal tried to scream it out and said, "Maudy, I don't understand, the doctors can't find the tumor. They took X-rays again and checked my throat but they couldn't find anything! What a miracle! The doctor told me, 'Minal, you were just here to show your pretty face. We don't really know what happened, but I am sure there will be an explanation for this. We apologize for this misunderstanding and inconvenience.'"

I was told by Kyra that Minal had followed her instructions the night before the anticipated surgery. She made a phone call to one of her children, plus an old friend. They were both very surprised, but equally delighted to hear from her.

I was so very happy for her and thankful she was given a chance to make things right with so many aspects of her life. It took a lot of courage for Minal to move forward and love herself with the help of her Aunt Nora. The moral was recognized.

Time passes very quickly, and I make sure I take time to enjoy the view. I am driven to let people know what they should pay attention to and what to avoid so they don't waste time. Get rid of the old grudge, whatever it may be, and clean out the mental closets.

Make things right with yourself and others and especially the people who are in spirit. I run into many people who are unable to make peace with someone who has entered heaven. We are going to get there eventually, so make peace with them here on earth. You will be able to enjoy life and live the time. Don't let time live you. It is never too late for peace.

Strength

Overcoming difficulties takes strength and love
Before it becomes hardship—we need to learn
     to be wise
We need to learn to recognize not to look
     at our weakness
Fear will block you from overcoming situations
To prevent hardship is to first overcome stress
     and frustrations
To leave fear behind
Is to make a change in your mind
The only way to keep negative energy at arm's length
Is to recognize life, willpower, love and your strength

On Courage: Maudisms to Remember

A Maudism (or Coat Hanger) is a phrase to memorize and hang on to when you are facing difficult situations.

Courage is strength and willpower
     ....
Courage is to look at your strength,
     never your weakness
     ....
Our Mind has a powerful energy
     ....
Our Mind can make us or break us
     ....
Live the time, don't let time live you

SIX

Forgiveness

Forgiveness is an element that everyone has to work on in their lives. We need to start by forgiving ourselves for anything that we have done to ourselves, and then we're able to forgive others. *Forgiveness is relief from resentment and rejection and allows you to go forward.*

The word forgiveness is one we'd often rather forget. Many painful memories may resurface. If we don't allow ourselves to forgive, we will consciously or subconsciously become prisoners of ourselves.

Gail and I notice when the element of forgiveness is mentioned during presentations, the body language in the room dramatically changes. A lot of "but, but, but" usually follows. As this word is repeated to me, I reply with, "The word 'but' is when we park ourselves on the couch. We either make the choice to use the remote control or get off the couch and get in control of ourselves."

The simple word "but" blocks us from moving forward in life because we are choosing to live in the past. It denies the peace in our hearts that we are looking for—and this is when we leave the door open for the domino effect of fear. Fear creates uncertainty and insecurity. To prevent this from happening, we can only make the choice of forgiveness, and it begins with ourselves.

Forgiveness also means that it is not what happens to us or is done to us, but what we can continue to do for others. We are here for our own goal, purpose, and destiny. We must learn to let go, get to know ourselves, and recognize ourselves. When we can acknowledge love and truth for ourselves, forgiveness is the remedy and will heal all wounds of life.

The next story will show you the impact of forgiveness on this person's life. Hopefully it will change how you look at and implement forgiveness in your own life.

Forgiveness from Many Mansions

People who live with deep-rooted anger have created a strong negative pattern within themselves that has no place for forgiveness. They have a strong negative energy field and are able to drag others down with them. A person in this state will never be happy unless they learn to forgive themselves.

When heaven places these people in front of me, sometimes it is necessary to shock them by letting them know where they went wrong on their journey. I have to take them back to where everything started, so they can see the cause and effect.

It's not only people on earth who ask for forgiveness. Those who are in heaven also ask for forgiveness from their loved ones here on earth.

During a presentation on dreams, we were introduced to Lauren, a very tall and articulate woman. She stated that she had been carrying a very heavy heart for over five years. Her friend Sandra, a thirty-seven-year-old police officer, was killed while on duty. About two weeks after Sandra's death, Lauren had a very poignant dream that haunted her. Sandra came to Lauren in a dream and said her death was an assisted murder. Lauren did not understand what Sandra meant.

I questioned Lauren about Sandra's state of mind. I said, "You were aware that Sandra had just broken up with someone and that she was depressed. Is that correct?" The answer was yes.

I continued, "Sandra had a gun and came face to face with her killer. She had the opportunity to pull the trigger, but chose not to. It was assisted murder because it was actually suicide." Lauren finally understood exactly what happened and what Sandra meant in the dream.

I explained to Lauren that there are many aspects to heaven, and since Sandra crashed the party, she now has to do earthly work from heaven. Crashing the party means that people who have committed suicide are not invited to heaven by God because it wasn't their time. Therefore, one must make amends. I told Lauren that Sandra was very pleased that she came to this presentation because now she could ask for forgiveness and could move forward in heaven.

However, Sandra, now able to work from heaven, needed Lauren's assistance to help someone from their old circle of friends who had thoughts about crossing over of their own free will. Sandra had to make right what was wrong because it was an injustice to body, mind, and soul. I also told Lauren that Sandra knew the person on earth that needed assistance, which is why she chose Lauren to deliver the apology to the loved ones Sandra left behind. It was an interesting and unique way for the people attending the presentation to view suicide, and in this case, solve the murder. It was like CSI from heaven!

There are many mansions in heaven for those who take their own lives. They are the people who have passed through life thinking that it wasn't worth the trouble. Now they have the opportunity to do earthly work from heaven and to correct the wrong that has been done.

Moving Forward

We often forget to say "I am sorry." While you should always forgive yourself first, it is important to forgive others for anything they did to you. If you don't consistently forgive yourself and others, you miss the true happiness in life that heaven intends for you. This brings me to a story about Lee, a Vietnamese woman.

The minute we walked in the door for a presentation, Lee was at my side asking questions. I assured her questions would be answered. Since she was so intense and verbal, I thought it best for her to sit and listen to the instructions and for the others to ask their questions.

Finally, we came to Lee. Through tears, she said, "Why me? I don't have anything. I have done everything for everyone. Why me?" She began to tell us of her difficult life growing up in Vietnam. She was recently divorced from her husband of thirty-six years. She described her life of being a maid who also attended to the needs of others while neglecting herself.

I was receiving messages and mentioning names of towns in Vietnam that were extremely difficult to pronounce. As Lee acknowledged them, there seemed to be a spark of hope in her eyes.

One of the people who had passed started interrupting me and the message was "Cuap Phong." I said to Lee, "Who is that?"

"I don't know!" she said.

Because this person was so persistent I said, "You must know this woman. She knows you!"

Suddenly, I got very dizzy and said to Gail, "This is awful. I'm so dizzy, like I'm in one of those tornadoes. I feel like I am inside of it." I was holding my head and holding on to the seat. I thought I was going to pass out. Gail grabbed my arm to steady me and said to Lee, "If you do not know who this person is, we will have to move on—or else Maudy will be sick."

Finally, Lee said, "That is my aunt. Cuap Phong. She hated me in life, and I didn't like her either."

"Thank goodness!" I said, not because of her difficult time in life, but for the person who had passed and now finally being acknowledged so I could deliver the message. Lee was expecting to hear what she wanted to hear, and I always say living with expectations is to live with disappointments. She did not want to hear from her aunt because of their past conflict. The world works in mysterious ways.

I proceeded to tell Lee there is only love in heaven and that her aunt wants to apologize to her for everything she did. She will now assist her in life. Because I sensed the anger and bitterness in Lee's voice, I told her to remember you can regret your speech, but never your silence. This was something her aunt did not do in life, and she wanted Lee to start looking at life in a new way. After the presentation, Lee accepted the message and the apology. She said that she was really going to work on the way she handled others from now on.

It was Cuap Phong's time to do earthly work from heaven. Forgiveness is a great thing and many times hard for many to act upon. Lee is now on the right track and will go forward and forgive.

Early Dismissal

Many of my daughter's friends know me and come to visit. Often, when I come home from the store, many cars are parked in my driveway. It's like a party. Of course, then I realize that they came for my guidance. The topics of discussion can be anything ranging from boy talk to career talk.

Upon one of these visits, the conversation turned serious. My daughters and their friends wanted to talk about their sixteen-year-old friend, Paul, who died in a car accident. The question these teens were stuck with was: "Why did he have to die?" These teens needed comfort and wanted to know how to deal with this terrible loss.

Everyone was very emotional as I explained what took place with the accident. It was especially hard for Alissa, Paul's sister. During the visit, Paul was very clear in relaying messages, and I felt that these teens needed to hear, learn, and live from what he had to say. I explained to them, "It's not about the one who died, it is about the one who lives. We are all here on borrowed time. It's not how long we live, but how we live."

Paul's lifetime was documented in heaven's archives and it was his time to go, but with a choice. I explained that Paul was saying "rebooted" over and over again. I knew this had nothing to do with the computer, but that's what you do to restart. I explained to the teens that he was given a chance to stay. However, he made a different choice. The paramedics resuscitated him, but he wanted to go.

Alissa burst into tears, and she acknowledged that no one knew that the paramedics tried to get him back to life. I said, "It was acknowledged that his choice was approved to go back home to heaven. You should see this as an early dismissal to do earthly work from heaven." I restated that we are all here on borrowed time, and that's why it's so important to live life to the fullest and to be ourselves.

Paul's friends were able to move on because they knew that Paul was happy and at peace. When you identify with this scenario, know that your loved ones have never left you. They will do earthly work from heaven and reboot your life.

Please Go Forward, I Am Fine!

Patty lost her twenty-four-year-old son, John, about six years ago in a car accident. She admits that she tends to live in the past. During a presentation, while delivering a message for Patty, John said, "When I passed, I did not know that I was dead! It happened so quickly that I knew I was not on earth anymore."

The message was delivered that even though he was very young when he passed, he had followed all seven of the elements of the spiritual law. I thought how cool is that? He then said, "All of you have to do this."

John's older sister, Shannon, was also in the room, and he acknowledged her. John said, "I want to show miracles to people in this room." He brought a boomerang to my attention. I asked Shannon, "Did someone in your family just go to Australia and bring back a boomerang?" Shannon was shocked because her fifteen-year-old daughter, Shelly, had just come back from Australia with a school friend. John said that he was with Shelly when she picked out the boomerang, and not to worry because he will continue to assist her on her entire life's journey.

John continued to tell everyone that he loved each of them very much. He added, "Always go to our creator first for assistance, and then ask for my assistance, too. I have been given permission to help family members." He continued to thank his mom and said he could not have had a better mother. He also asked her to go forward in life because he is enjoying himself and wants her to do the same.

I noticed a man was standing next to John. The man wasn't saying anything or communicating in any way. I brought this to the attention of Patty, as I wasn't sure who he was. He was just standing there. I wondered if he was John's biological father. This brought Patty and Shannon to laughter, and Patty said, "Well, even in life, his father was not able to communicate. So in death it doesn't surprise me that he is the same."

John was really talkative and wanted Shannon to speak to William, a good friend of his who is still alive, and tell him "All will be well!" Apparently there was difficulty in this individual's life and John wanted to reassure him that everything would be okay.

According to Patty, John had a strange sense of humor and won many sports awards. I reassured them that John had received an award in heaven because even though he was very young when he passed, he really did live the spiritual law.

Shannon made a final statement that she realized many things after John's death, and one thing she learned was that God has put us here to lift each other up, not to put each other down. She misses her brother's positive attitude and now knows that miracles will happen with following the seven elements. This is just another example of the fact that it is never too late to start again and get back on the right spiritual track.

John's last message to me, for the time being, was to reassure his mother that he was fine and for her to please go forward and stop living in the past. He lives in the present and wants her to do the same.

Sometimes we tend to think that because our loved ones have passed, they do not see how we have handled their passing and how we live our lives. This is the ultimate example of someone who will assist his family members to go forward in life. John was certainly aware of what took place in the lives of his mother and his sister.

For me, this was a very comforting encounter with two people who loved John in life and continue to love him. It was reassurance from heaven that truly, all will be well!

Marjorie's Story

The following story is about Marjorie, and perhaps you might identify with her story. I had received a phone call from Marjorie, who had to go to Washington, DC, because her father had passed away. She asked me, "I am so concerned. Where do people go when they cross over if they have done bad things in life? I have read so many books in different religions. I studied theology and am totally confused now that my father has passed. I was with my father when he took his last breath and I held his hand and prayed that the Lord would forgive him. In his lifetime, he had done bad things to me and to other people. Where is he going to go?" She continued to explain: "My father was lying in bed so very helpless. His last words to me was that he asked me to forgive him. I did."

I explained to Marjorie that God is very good to us. He gives us numerous chances and choices. We make choices in life that either work with us or against us. When life works against us, we have a choice to restructure and make changes. Usually we take the easy way out and dwell on the problem, not the solution. When we dwell on the problem, we create stress, frustration, and depression. We will not be in control of our own life, and at some point, we would rather control other people's lives on their particular life journey.

As I was talking to Marjorie, she was crying and I calmed her down. I told her, "It was your father who sentenced himself through his actions. He did things in life that were wrong, but look at the end of his life. You were both given a chance to forgive. It is all reported and recorded in heaven's journal. You forgave each other. How powerful is that?" I explained that it is not what has been done to you, but what you will continue to do for yourself and for others.

For many people, forgiveness is a very difficult concept to accept, especially if they've experiences any type of abuse or cruelty. Strong faith will bring peace and ease in time.

I explained to Marjorie that in her father's life journey, he disrespected himself, so he disrespected others in a negative way. Further, I explained that her father will be evaluated in heaven and be presented with the opportunity to bring justice where he brought injustice to mind, body, and spirit when he was on earth. In Marjorie's case, her father did not live up to love. Her father will know the meaning of the word love for whatever mission he is assigned, and then he will be able to do earthly work from heaven.

Marjorie then asked, "What can I do?" I said, "Marjorie, see it as your job to stay vigilant and be connected to faith. Recognize where you can make positive changes with yourself and for yourself. Simply pray for your father and live continuously with forgiveness."

She then said, "I feel like you took away a burden that I have been carrying with me for a long time. I think now I have to come to a decision, and the choice is that I have to let go."

Since that first phone call, Marjorie calls from time to time and keeps me updated on how she is doing. She is truly touching base with what she needs to do for herself. What a wonderful growing experience for her. She is now able to let go and enjoy life. She prays for her dad and leaves it in the hands of God. Forgiveness is necessary for all of us to free ourselves.

You Say Apples, I Hear Pears

How often does this happen? Too often. You say one thing and I hear the other. These can be the times when we are so preoccupied with our thoughts that we lack focus on life itself. Most often this results in only a minor inconvenience, but there are times when this situation leads to an escalating argument that causes emotional harm.

In our daily lives, we sometimes go 150 miles per hour. We need to realize that we can all make mistakes, such as, when the "mis"-chain reaction takes place—like a mis-understanding, mis-placed, mis-calculation, and the list goes on. In other words, this will eventually work against us if we don't step on our "brakes" and say, "Enough!" Then it is time to sit back and relax and rejuvenate.

In a flash of a second, not being on the same frequency of a conversation can cause a misunderstanding. This "static" in being receptive can create a negative response. However, avoiding this static in communication is possible, but learning to listen attentively takes a lot of time and practice. The payoff is that you will receive the message exactly as the sender intended. We all have experienced this type of situation. Once we apologize for our inattentiveness, we can be forgiven. However, when the reaction is a negative response, it can escalate into judgment day!

Lack of Communication

Sheila and Bob had a definite lack of communication. They certainly were plagued with the "I say apples, you hear pears" syndrome. The love for each other was still there. However, when they talked to each other, they heard the other's voice but did not listen. This can go on for a long time in a relationship without incident, until one day the bucket overflows and one person might think of leaving—unless there is a conscientious effort to change. This will also include forgiveness because there is hurt through words placed upon each other.

When Sheila and I first met, she asked, "Maudy, how should I control myself in a situation when I am trying to get my point across? It seems that every time Bob and I get into a discussion, it escalates into a yelling and screaming match. It drives me crazy. I really don't think I can handle this anymore. I don't know if I can forgive him. However, I am still in love with him."

Sheila continued: "He has little patience and really jumps all over me when I misunderstand him. When he told me we were having company over on Saturday, I thought he said Sunday. Well, because I misunderstood the day, I had to prepare everything at the last minute. Obviously this caused me total frustration, and I was totally frazzled. So was he."

I tried to explain to Sheila that when you let life live you—you lose touch with yourself and the world. Then, this causes you to go through life computerized. Your mind is set on "automatic pilot" and programmed to do what you expect it to do. So when you make a mistake, the world seems to turn against you. The world expects you to be "logged in" and subconsciously you put yourself on pause. While your mind is wandering—and you may have even put yourself on mute—you are not on the same frequency. Therefore, you will have to practice forgiveness for yourself and others because of your unconscious state of mind.

I did ask Sheila to have her husband call me because I was being nudged by a spirit in heaven that wanted to assist him with his marriage to Sheila and in life. So Sheila gave the message to Bob.

Bob called me about a week later, and immediately I was getting angel whispers from his college friend Drew, who had passed as a result of a car accident. I presented Bob with options and left him choices to make in regard to his relationship with Sheila. Further, it became apparent that he must embrace his faith and forgiveness so he could continue to live his life from day to day.

Several months later, Sheila and Bob called me again. They wanted to let me know their progress. Bob said: "Maudy, we're getting back on track and really want to thank Drew and you for the assistance." Then Sheila continued and said "I even joined an aerobics class and feel great. It isn't easy to reverse negative energy into positive energy and apply forgiveness, but I am working on it, because I know we can and will make it as a couple."

Life is Cause and Effect

The easiest way we can help ourselves is to be willing to step on our own brakes, which simply means take it easy. Life is cause and effect, and in order to recognize cause, you need to be fully aware and recognize your thoughts. Further, once you gain this recognition, remember to reverse negative thoughts into positive. Thoughts are powerful—for words and deeds arise only from thoughts. The mind can make you or break you. Also, it is very important in situations like this to get our point across—not ourselves. When we give ourselves time to rest and simmer down, we will energize our minds and be fully aware of the circumstances that surround us.

Suddenly in Overdrive

Being in overdrive always needs a correction. I can attest to that personally. Anyone who has ever had a job knows that many times, not only do you go on automatic pilot—you go into overdrive because of everything on your mind.

When I worked in a doctor's office, I was preparing patient files for the morning appointments, and my friends at work were discussing their personal problems with me. During the conversations, their emotions were running really high. As I comforted and encouraged them, the telephone started to ring. My thoughts were still with the conversation of my fellow workers.

When I answered the phone, my thoughts were still with the friend in the office, who was now in tears! Then I said to the man on the telephone: "Of course, you can make an appointment. Let me check your information in the computer." I continued: "Sir, did I spell your name correctly: first name Duane, last name Scott?" Before he could answer I stated, "Sir, I can't find your name in the computer—you are not registered. When was your last office visit?"

Suddenly, the office became very quiet. I looked at my coworkers and no one said a word—they just looked at me in a strange manner. I repeated my question to the gentlemen on the phone. "Sir, are you still there?" "Yes," he replied. He then said: "You spelled my name correctly, but how did you know my name is Duane Scott? I did not give you my name at all."

I answered by saying: "Sir, you did tell me your name." His answer: "No Miss, I did not, I only asked if I could make an appointment. I am a new patient. Therefore, I am not yet registered in the computer, which is why you could not find my name. I am curious though. Who are you?"

I felt totally "busted," and obviously this was a predicament for me. I felt my blood pressure rise and my face turning red. I had to reconnect with my thoughts in my mind and undo this situation. Quickly, I responded, "Sir, have you heard the saying, 'You say apples and I hear pears'?" I know this was one of those conversations that absolutely made no sense to him, however I felt that I had to protect myself by switching gears immediately. I did not want to explain what just took place. It was his father who had passed away that was giving me angel whispers while on the phone. The gentleman on the phone "woke" me up by making me aware of the conversation and brought to my attention that I did not know him.

The message certainly became very clear to me—that I have to be totally alert at all times and maintain focus on life around me. Situations like this can cause interesting predicaments in my social life. And this certainly was not the opportune time or place to explain angel whispers—while working in a doctor's office.

Yes, I did make an appointment for Mr. Duane Scott on my day off!

Dad Is Fine

In my world, everyone is "familiar" and the most comical situations can take place with the "absence of mind." It can get out of control when the supernatural takes over the subconscious mind. In other words, I am not conscious or in control of my thoughts. This has occurred when I approach people that I have never met before—but I thought I knew. I am very excited and happy to see them and just start a conversation—like I've known them for years.

One day, while still working for the doctor, I had returned from the post office ready to go to work. During my lunch, I had gone to mail a Christmas package and was amazed at how much it cost to mail something overseas compared to the actual cost of the present.

So while my mind was left with these thoughts, I walked into the doctor's office and looked at the woman standing in front of the registration window. I walked straight up to her and greeted this woman as if I've known her forever. I asked her if her father had recovered from heart surgery and if he was still living in Estaban or had he already moved to Paris? I heard myself "rambling" on with this conversation, but was not fully aware as to what was actually happening.

While this was taking place, I saw the absolute look of surprise and astonishment on the faces of my colleagues.

The woman was very fixated upon this conversation, and I know she was thinking: "I must know her—but how does she know me?" Then she looked at me and said, "Yes, my father is doing well, and now lives in Paris. It is so nice of you to remember where we lived." Then with hesitation in her voice, she asked, "You didn't forget my name?" I answered, "Of course not, I was so happy your parents named you Maradeah." She suddenly embraced me and hugged me and with this action I woke up. Again, I was busted. I didn't want to frighten her and decided to tactfully excuse myself from the reception area of the office.

This woman, Maradeah, was apparently from the Middle East and had also come to register as a new patient. The comical part was when she addressed me and said, "You know, I totally forgot your name. What is it? When did we last meet?"

What she really meant was: "Who are you? How do we know each other?" With my stomach in a knot, I answered, "My name is Maudy. Remember, we met a long, long time ago. Oh, those good old days; we had such fun." While I was saying this, I recognized that I needed to "reconnect with my mind" and get back to the awareness of my environment. I told myself, "Maudy, you better get out of this conversation—fast!" Quickly, I moved toward the door to the back office.

In this type of situation, when I am not alert and the supernatural ability takes control—afterwards, I am aware that the "wavelength" is set in direct contact with the angels' grapevine—and the angel whispers keep on coming! When I stay alert and focus and live with self-awareness, I am able to block this from happening and maintain control of my surroundings and me.

Cruise Control

In the carousel of life, it is very important to make time and find the love for you—by living in the moment and being fully aware. After all, it is necessary to control your mind and make time for you. If you used to write in a journal—then make time to write. Whatever gave you comfort previously, begin doing that again. Recognize and confront your feelings. Be more alert regarding what you are saying. Live in the now. If it sounds negative, reverse it into positive. Forgive yourself first…then the world.

When we exercise our body and it gets tired, we need to rest. When the mind is overworked, it automatically switches to "cruise control." When this happens, we doze off and allow it to control us! To reach happiness and inner peace, you need to practice the power of positive thinking through prayer and recognize the simplicity of life. Life is simple; we make it difficult! Learn to "simplify your life."

To avoid the phrase, "You say apples, I hear pears," you must tap into the voice from above. With faith and forgiveness, you will be given the daily affirmations to go forward.

In this world of wireless electronics, there is much static, and we may even experience "a crash in our computer." However, all you need to do is listen. Heaven is always online to ask us: "Can you hear me now?"

Inhale and Exhale
You cannot make room for the future
When you live in the past
…Inhale…Exhale
You cannot see the beauty of nature when you feel…
Nothing will last
…Inhale…Exhale
Embrace life and feel the rain on your skin
…Inhale…Exhale
Give yourself time and let the sunshine in
…Inhale…Exhale
Whatever you do
Follow through with Love for you
…Inhale…Exhale

On Forgiveness: Maudisms to Remember

A Maudism (or Coat Hanger) is a phrase to memorize and hang on to when you are facing difficult situations.

Forgiveness is relief from resentment and rejection and...allows you to go forward

....

Forgiveness means, it is not what has been done to us, but what we can continue to do for ourselves and others

....

It is not about the one who died, it is about the one who lives

....

Strong faith will bring peace and ease

....

Forgiveness is necessary to free ourselves

....

Forgive yourself first and then the world

SEVEN

Belief

Belief is a beautiful element that will lighten your life. It is not about religion, but the confidence to believe in yourself. I often say, "To believe is to achieve and to receive." This simply means that with faith, you will reach your goal and you will receive your heart's desires.

Belief is having faith in what heaven has planned. Once you believe in yourself, you will believe in your higher power and miracles will begin to happen in your life. You will reach anything in life and conquer life's obstacles.

This chapter also includes the belief in angels, how they work in our lives, and how they may appear in human form. This belief validates that angels are supernatural and help you know that you are always protected and never alone.

Angels are here to comfort and guide; understanding and acknowledging their existence will help your belief system.

Dreams fall under belief and are another solid way of heaven transmitting personal messages directly to each individual. Although sometimes cryptic, dreams assist you in your daily life. Dreams are not simply part of your imagination. They are real. Always remember that dreams are a guide to understanding the supernatural and how you can benefit from the messages that are sent to you.

Let's see how you can put belief back into your life and pass it on to others.

I admire all the people who explain my work and me to others. It takes courage for people to introduce someone to my world and me. Many times, skeptics will turn away when they hear the explanation of angel whisperer. It is the unknown that makes people insecure. I also let them know that it takes only one encounter, and as they challenge me, I will then challenge them. The funny thing is, once people know me, they come to recognize me as a walking information desk. Through the message of belief, people will see their miracles happen and doors open up in ways they cannot imagine.

Heavenly Navigation

Bonnie worked at a local florist shop. I recognized that she was somewhat lost and needed guidance. Bonnie told me she didn't know if there was a supreme being; however, she suspected that there might be angels. I gave her the explanation, "If you believe in angels, you might want to consider a higher being because He created them."

Bonnie was quick to tell me that she was skeptical about anyone who talked about heaven because she had bad experiences in her life. She admitted that belief in any of its forms simply wasn't there for her.

I knew that this woman needed a lot of help.

Bonnie became very emotional when I gave her a message from her father, who had passed. I informed her that she needed to move to Florida to be with the family. She wasn't sure why Florida, except that she did have a grown son and a grandson living there.

She was puzzled, but I told her to stick with her dad's instructions, as heaven would show her miracles. Bonnie was giving me reasons why she couldn't move, and one of them was the fear of her house not being sold.

I told her that I have to say what I hear, and that she needed to move to Florida to be with her son and grandson, and all would fall into place. I also said that God would show her his love for her, and all it takes is for her to have the belief.

Bonnie called a couple weeks later and said she had taken her dad's advice to put the house on the market. The house sold within a month and she moved to Florida.

Once Bonnie established herself in a town next to her son, her grandson Ross asked if he could live with her before going off to college. Ross felt the need to get to know his grandma. Bonnie thought it was a great idea. Ross lived with her for about nine months before going off to school in New Hampshire.

During this time frame, Bonnie called me and was pleased that she got to know her family better and was starting to understand the word "belief." She even decided to join a local church.

Her faith became stronger all because of her belief in a supreme being and herself. Bonnie was sad that her grandson had to go off to college, but was glad to have had the opportunity to know him.

Ross was in New Hampshire for one week when he was struck and killed by a drunken driver. The entire family was devastated. Ross was only twenty years old.

Bonnie called and asked us for prayers. I spoke directly to her, and she said that without knowing a supreme being and having belief in Him, she didn't know how she would have coped or even survived through this tough time.

My message of belief was again delivered. This time it was not for me to know the reason why, just to deliver the message. I was not aware that her grandson would pass. I only knew that she had to move to Florida and be with the family.

Living the Seven Elements

The seven elements are rather simple, but can be very difficult to live, especially when you need to practice putting them into your daily life and actually live them. And it requires practice. You will find that when you teach people what you have learned, you come to the realization that you are learning from your own voice. For the people placed on your path, this information will enlighten and empower their lives, so then they will illuminate their hearts and those of others.

The following story is a good example of someone who was willing to change his life in a big way.

Danny was recently placed on my path. He had been married for thirty-one years and took anti-anxiety pills for depression for twenty-five years. His wife did not know how to handle his depression, and they were thinking about a separation. I made an appointment to meet Danny at a restaurant. Well, that first appointment never took place, and neither did the second. Danny cancelled both of them. He finally found his courage and we met at a local restaurant.

When I arrived at the restaurant, I noticed a construction worker leaning up against the far wall outside the restaurant. I knew this was Danny, although he did not look at me. I noticed the familiar nervous demeanor in his posture and body language. I walked inside the restaurant and waited ten minutes. Danny still hadn't come in. I was rather curious as to where he was, so I looked out the window to see if he was still standing there. When I turned around, there was Danny standing right behind me. Danny is twice my size, so it was rather comical that I bumped directly into him. He was still nervous and without words he mouthed his name, and I mouthed back mine. It was embarrassing for us to bump into each other, but funnier that neither of us said our names out loud. At this point, I was relieved the ice had been broken so we could begin.

His cell phone kept going off during our conversation. He told me that he couldn't miss a business call and apologized for the interruption. Finally, after several rings, he decided it would be best to simply shut off the phone. I was pleased because cell phones tend to disrupt my thought process.

I started off about explaining who I am and what I do. I told Danny, "To know where you are going is to first know where you have been."

Danny's father, who had passed four years ago, informed me of when the depression started with his son. I had to let him know when the misunderstanding with his father began. I described his father, and dropped the name Troy. This was Danny's father's middle name. His father asked Danny for forgiveness, and Danny started to become emotional. He started to cry, so I grabbed his hand. His hand was twice as big as mine, and I thought, "Okay, I have to do what I have to do to comfort him." The waitress came to me and asked if everything was okay. I answered, "Sure, we are just fine. As good as it can be for now." Danny was still very emotional, and this is a familiar scenario for me.

I realized that through his tears, a big part of his past, his luggage had already been taken away. This was a man who made the choice to live through his work and ignore everything else. During our conversation, he did not even look at the time, and over two hours had already passed. It took him that long to come to peace with himself.

I gave him a big hug and could see that he could now let go of the past. While looking for a handkerchief, Danny subconsciously turned on his cell phone. When he did this, it immediately rang, startling both of us. He threw the cell phone into the air, and I caught it and immediately gave it back to him. I said, "Tell your wife I said hi and take her to the mountains." It was his wife on the phone, and he looked at me in awe.

I took this opportunity to silently leave the restaurant and got the familiar goosebumps. This for me is confirmation of a beautiful new beginning for Danny. Danny will now be able to live life instead of life living him.

Danny's father was able to give Danny the choice to make peace with himself and fulfill his mission by doing heavenly work here on earth. Seven days later, Danny's wife Tara called to tell me that she and the rest of Danny's family recognized a big change in him. Danny announced to Tara that he didn't need a psychologist anymore and was ready to cut down the anti-anxiety medication under the doctor's supervision. Tara was very emotional and speechless through this whole experience. In this short time, they were able to mend their relationship and spend quality time together to catch up on lost time.

The most beautiful part was that Danny booked a trip to the mountains with his wife. Tara and Danny had never had a vacation because of his depression, and they never wanted to be that close. I told Tara that the cake has not lost its frosting and she started to laugh. I left the conversation with these words, "Faith doesn't have any doubt. Faith has no fear."

Within two weeks of our initial visit, Tara and Danny arranged a home presentation. I couldn't believe the person I came face to face with. I thought it was a different man. Not only was this man smiling, he was beaming. Danny's self-love was becoming evident to me, and I knew that he and his wife were doing very well. He was ready to help others. This to me cannot be measured in words. It is just a blessing for me to witness.

In the above story, all seven elements came into play. There was love, honor, and respect of his wife, who was willing to keep the marriage going. She was patient because she knew her husband was a good man. Forgiveness of his past, through an apology from his dad, helped Danny go forward. Now both he and his wife were able to go forward through belief in themselves and a higher power to make their way a more peaceful existence.

To Believe Is to See

Heaven works in mysterious, miraculous, and magical ways. In my journey, I'm frequently tested and challenged. I usually begin presentations by saying that I am not here for entertainment, but to deliver a serious message. What you do with the message is up to you.

Gail and I were invited to a large presentation in a very affluent area of the Northeast with many people we knew, and some we didn't. Everyone was very friendly and we were ready to go. However, I whispered to Gail ahead of time, I felt this group had a lot skeptics—more than usual. I explained if they wanted entertainment, this is not the place, because we have serious angel messages for each of them. So we began with Zack.

Zack came with his wife, Silvia. Both of them were extremely skeptical. Through the angels' information, I already knew that this man had turned away from prayer. Zack, sitting with folded arms, blurted out: "What can you tell me about my cousin Corey?" I paused for a moment because I didn't like what I sensed. I said, "I smell smoke and something burning." I did not tell him that I was becoming nauseated because of the smell of burned flesh.

I looked directly at him, and he and his wife immediately burst into tears. I asked Zack what happened. He explained that twenty-five years ago his cousin, who was sixteen, died in a fiery car crash.

At this time, all eyes were on Zack, and there wasn't a dry eye in the room. I told Zack what message was being delivered: "Heaven is requesting a prayer."

Zack's attitude became defensive, and with anger in his voice he said, "Why do I need to pray? Heaven hasn't done anything for me. I am always doing things for other people. I don't need anyone."

After giving him a moment, I continued, "'We know you've helped many people and that you have dealt with many losses as well. It is not about the one who died. It is about you, the one left behind."

I continued, "Your cousin appreciates everything you've done for him, and our creator has given him approval to help you. All it takes is prayer, and this prayer is for you. You turned away from heaven and our creator. This is why you had to come to this presentation. Now your cousin can help you make things right with yourself through prayer."

By this time, Zack was completely overpowered. His defensive and skeptical attitude disappeared. I turned to the audience and asked, "Who is Jewish or Hebrew?" No one raised a hand. Then Zack came forward. "I am part Jewish," he said with a softer voice.

I looked at him and said, "Good. This message is especially for you, as it comes straight from heaven. Corey is mentioning the word *malakh*. It is Jewish or Hebrew; can you tell me what it means?" Zack didn't know. I told him that it was important for him to find out the meaning of this word because it was a message for him.

After the presentation, as I was about to leave, Zack and his wife, with tears still in their eyes, embraced me. I whispered, "Time to get busy, then all will be well!" He knew that I meant it was time to get busy with prayer.

Later, I was informed that the word *malakh* means "messenger, prophet, and reflection." Corey was doing earthly work from heaven as a messenger bringing prophecy through a reflection back with Zack as his mission.

The Doubting Thomas Club

At a presentation in a very large hotel setting, we had been invited by Mr. Christmas, a very affluent man with a lot of influential people in his circle. I wasn't aware until later that Mr. Christmas did not tell any of his invited guests about me or Gail. After the presentation we were informed that there were people from Broadway, Wall Street, and script writers and magazine writers in the group. To me, people are people. We work with the poorest to the richest. Their problems are the same.

Before we started, a man approached Gail and really started to grill her. I realized that he thought Gail was the angel whisperer! I walked behind this man, smiled at Gail, and sat down. I was rather tickled. Gail was doing a good job of answering his questions as they spoke for at least ten minutes. Finally, the man ran out of questions and took a seat in the audience. I immediately said to Gail, "Let's keep this man for last." We knew we were in for a difficult time. Everyone was ready to test us, but I was ready for whatever they were going to say.

Sometimes I find that people do not understand the concept of "to believe is to see." This is evident in the spiritual world, yet many people have difficulty. God is the supreme supernatural being and angels are pure spirits that are supernatural and very real. Therefore, understanding my gift shouldn't be difficult for those of faith. Correct? Well, let me explain. During this intense presentation, I finally came face to face with a theologian. Yes, he was the man grilling Gail. He was forceful and totally skeptical, somewhat like a doubting Thomas. Because of his strong body language, we thought it best to let him observe and listen to the teachings, and, indeed, he should be last. This would give him the opportunity to listen to the other encounters and see how heaven works for everyone.

Just before getting to Lance, our resident doubting Thomas, there was such a poignant encounter that everyone was still crying. The tears had flowed for some time. I thought that this might enlighten him a little bit.

Finally, I got to Lance. With arms folded against his chest, he said, "Well, I don't particularly need your help like these other people. I don't have problems like them." Everyone in the room immediately turned and glared at

Lance. To my surprise, he continued questioning but it was in a continuous story form, and he just kept going.

I was sitting with Gail in front of this very large crowd, and I turned to her with my teeth clenched, smiling, and lips not moving, and said, "I don't understand what he is asking or saying."

"Neither do I," she answered with the same smile with her teeth clenched. It was one of those times I knew I would eventually be able to get into the conversation, once he allowed it. I held my ground, smiling and patiently waiting.

Finally, still with his arms folded, he said, "Well, if you have a message from Shakespeare, Aristotle, Socrates, or Jesus Christ, I'll listen!" I was thinking to myself, "But do they want to talk with him?" I was still smiling and waiting. Then he threw his arms up in the air and said, "Okay, just tell me whatever you have for me!"

I said, "You are constantly searching, and the answer is right in front of you. It is in the Book of Revelation." He listened intently.

More information was being delivered. I asked him if he had been reading a red book from his bookshelf. I was being informed that he had just read it and had it in his hands. He did acknowledge that he reads a lot, and I was being advised to tell him to go back to this particular book, and it would be on the third or fourth shelf on his bookcase. "Please go to the red book and go to page 20, three-quarters of the way down, below the hieroglyphics, and your answer is there."

At this point, Lance wasn't quite sure if he wanted to end this conversation. The information was still continuing for me because the next question that was presented for me to ask was: "Do you still like what you brought back from Tibet, and are you still interested?" He looked puzzled, and for the first time in our entire encounter, he couldn't figure out what that was.

Then his friend nudged him and said, "It is your wife. You brought her back from Tibet!" Everyone broke into laughter, including Lance.

I am hoping that the doubting Thomas is not doubting anymore. I know there were many hours of discussion with his friend, who hosted the presentation, of what had taken place. Because of his nature, I know Lance will continue to search and research for the meaning of life. However, I believe the veil was being lifted, and even with his skepticism, he knew that what was delivered was indeed true. Simplicity of life is all that matters, and even in the world of theologians, it takes time to think about the phrase "to believe is to see."

It Only Takes One Encounter

Another group of individuals I enjoy working with is the psychologists. I know I am a puzzle to them. However, many of them are really open to me—not at first, of course, but after they have that encounter. I always say, "It only takes one encounter."

Gail and I were invited to speak to a group of teens at a group home. We got permission from everyone involved beforehand. There was one young teen there, Jack, who had not contacted his psychologist, who was also his guardian, so I wasn't sure if I would be able to talk with him. When we arrived at the group home, I was given the phone to speak directly to Jack's psychologist, Dr. Lewis. He had a few questions, but soon everything was okay.

We gave an uplifting talk to these young people, and then I was allowed a few minutes with each teen on an individual basis. After we had left, I heard from two of the psychologists on site, plus Dr. Lewis. They wanted to know what positive messages were delivered because each of the teens was in a very uplifted mood.

Jack, in particular, kept telling Dr. Lewis that he knew he had to close the door to the past and go forward. I had explained to Jack that it was time for him to let go of the luggage from the past, and life would change for him.

This simple explanation annoyed Dr. Lewis, as he had been working with this young man for over six months. The doctor told me later that this was the first time Jack had opened up to anyone. His annoyance was that it was to a complete stranger and not even a psychologist!

Because of our visit and the interest of Dr. Lewis, we started to give presentations to his fellow psychologists and psychiatrists on a regular basis—all because of angels' information, which each one of these professional people was now interested in understanding.

Dr. Lewis explained to me later that he was amazed because the fundamentals of cognitive-behavioral therapy and psychoanalysis were actually applied. I did not know exactly what he meant because I was simply delivering the messages as I heard them. We both laughed and now he is a good friend of ours. He also now understands the phrase "to believe is to see," because he certainly has done so.

To me, the above two stories are the perfect example of a doubting Thomas club. It is human nature to doubt, and the reason why I am put in the paths of doubters is always a surprise to me, as it is to them.

I have come to the conclusion that they needed to sharpen their level of spirituality and belief in a higher power. Once this is done, they can actually believe in themselves, which is self-realization. And they will see miracles happen.

The tool used to sharpen their spirituality is the very gift I have been given. This actually comes when I come into their world as the complete stranger, an angel whisperer, who delivers messages from those who have passed to assist those left behind on their life's journey.

Recognize the Angel Beside You

Angels are the links by which I receive messages from those who have passed. I have my special relationship with them, but anyone is capable of communicating with angels. It doesn't take a gift to ask for their help or advice. At times, we don't even know we have encountered an angel. They are special beings and are on a mission to help us and spread love.

Angel Appearance

I have been privileged to see an angel only once. It was an incredible experience and only lasted for a flash of a second. I witnessed an enormous angel, close to eight feet tall, coming behind a child as she entered a room. It had very big wings that were feathery and beautiful. I was made aware at that time that this particular child was protected by this angel and this protection would continue throughout her life's journey.

It was simply a reminder to me, as in all angelic language, that this was a gift to me to cherish. I am also aware that not everyone sees an angel. However, you might feel the presence of an angel, and that is also a wonderful treasure.

Explanation of Angels

Gail will now explain angels and their purpose.

Angels are pure spirits who have specific missions to accomplish. We are most familiar with our guardian angels who protect us. Maudy refers to messages she receives as angel whispers because the angels are the links to your loved ones. This is explained on a regular basis, but sometimes people forget about the angels because of the impact of the message. Many people do not recognize the angel that walks beside them or is placed in front of them.

An angel is not a human being, and no human being can become an angel here on earth. Angels are sent to work through humans or flown to earth on heaven's behalf to fulfill a mission.

Many times we refer to our loved ones in spirit as angels; however, we must remember that is an affectionate human term, and only God can create angels. One thing I'd like to point out is that after a person has passed, it also means they have successfully fulfilled their life's purpose and mission. After passing the heavenly evaluations between the soul and God, then we will see what type of wings we might get. They could even be angel wings.

I have learned so much since I have been standing next to Maudy. There are certain things you question as you are growing up, and I wonder if some of my life experiences are really supernatural. I felt my faith was strong before, and getting to know Maudy has made it only stronger. What I am now able to recognize is the deeper understanding and wisdom gained by each and every supernatural event. Life and its experiences have become richer and empowered me with more self-realization than I thought ever possible. This is all as a result of working side by side with Maudy.

I thank her and God and His angels for having her placed on my path.

Angels are always on assignment for heaven. They accompany us from our birth and stay with us our entire lives until we return to our heavenly home. These unique supernatural beings are here to show us the answers to our prayers and assist us on life's journey. We want to let you recognize this wonderful supernatural opportunity and how to enjoy your angels. Let's see how these wonderful angels have come to others we have encountered along the way.

Angels in Human Form

Our friend Edna lives in the northeastern area of the United States and is always assisting others in whatever way she can. After her children were grown, she decided it was time to assist people in hospice care. She went through the training and was given her first assignment. Her main concern was that she had never driven much in her very busy city community. The roads were narrow and often congested. However, she decided she would use her courage and conquer this fear.

It was a Monday morning and she got out the address that the hospice had given her. It was about eight miles from her house. Once she got to the area, she couldn't find the house. She drove around, trying to find the house, but she had turned herself around so much that she had to stop and park the car. She wasn't prone to getting anxious but this was unnerving her a bit because she had already been on the road for an hour!

It was midmorning and not many people were out and about in the neighborhood. She noticed a man standing near a bus stop and decided to approach him for directions. She said, "Hello, I am volunteering for hospice and am looking for 24 Plymouth Street and a Mr. Thomas Dougherty." The man replied, "Oh, I've known Tom for years. I live right across the street from him and his wife Sue. You are only about a mile away. Simply take this left and one more left and you'll find their house on the right hand side of the street."

Edna noticed that this man's hair was shining like silver in the sunlight, and he had an incredible welcoming smile with beautiful, bright white teeth. As she was driving away, she thought about what funny things we remember about people and how thankful she was to find this helpful gentlemen.

Edna arrived at the house, met Sue and Tom, and apologized for being late. She told them about getting lost and the man who gave her directions. Both Sue and Tom looked at Edna. Sue said, "Oh, you must be mistaken." Edna replied, "Oh, he was so helpful. I just can't begin to tell you how much help he was to me." Sue said, "Edna, no one lives across the street from us. There is a park, and it has been there for years. Look for yourself." Edna looked out their living room window and was speechless. Sure enough, there was a very large park! In fact, the entire left-hand side of the street was covered with acres of parkland.

Edna was taken aback, but continued to visit and get acquainted with her new hospice patient. She passed the bus stop on the way home and was hoping to see this man again, but he was not there. Once she was home, Edna reviewed the events of the day and her encounter with the man. She remembered his words, how kind he was, his silver white hair, and that welcoming smile. Edna realized that she had indeed been in contact with an angel who helped her find her hospice patient.

Affirmation from Heaven

When you encounter an angel, you usually realize what has happened after the fact and get the familiar goosebumps, which are an affirmation from heaven of what has taken place.

I told Maudy about an incredible experience I had. My distant relative Damien passed early in January 2008, and I was unable to go to the funeral. Damien had a sad life full of things he was unable to rise above. When he was sixteen years old, he was riding his motorcycle and his friend Ross was his passenger. They were not paying attention and fast approaching a stop sign. Damien had to stop quickly, and both he and Ross were thrown from the bike. Ross died upon impact with the pavement and Damien walked away with only a few scratches. This was the beginning of a life-long struggle for Damien.

I worked at the local hospital and saw Damien about two weeks after the accident. We embraced and I said, "Damien, I am sorry for your loss. Please make sure to go to the counselor and get the help you need." Damien, who still had scars on his face from the accident, looked at me and said, "Don't worry, Gail. I am just fine." That was the last time that I saw him for quite some time.

Because Damien was unable to rise above that, he turned to drugs and alcohol. His parents, sisters, brothers, and the rest of the family often did not know where he was—sometimes for months at a time. We were all accustomed to praying for Damien.

The night before Damien died, he called his father and asked to be taken to the emergency room. He did not feel well and thought he had bronchitis. Once Damien was checked in, the doctor told Damien's dad that the bronchitis had turned into pneumonia, so they were going to keep Damien in the hospital for a few days to run tests. It was about 10 p.m., so Damien's father went home.

At seven the following morning, the hospital phoned Damien's parents to inform them that Damien had passed away. It was a shock to everyone. The memorial service for Damien was planned in January. However, due to heavy snows in the Northeast, he was not buried until exactly five months to the day that he passed.

Since I was unable to go to the burial, I went to a local church in the morning to pray for Damien and then came home. Damien was being buried at 1 p.m., which was the exact time I was in the kitchen preparing lunch for my dad, when I heard the sound of a cuckoo clock. I had the television on, but the volume was on low and was tuned to CNN, so I knew that wasn't it. I went into my formal living room and looked at the cuckoo clock on the wall. The pendulum was moving back and forth. This was quite a surprise because this clock had not run or been wound in the past twelve years because it was so noisy.

This clock was not near a window, nor an open door, and it was two rooms away from my ninety-three-year-old father. I stood there watching that pendulum in a daze for some time, trying to figure out how and why it started running. I then heard Damien's voice: "Don't worry, Gail. I am just fine!" This time I believed him!

The clock kept running, and I had to physically stop the pendulum from moving from side to side. It was Damien's angel moving the pendulum to let me know that he was okay and now at peace. I had prayed Damien would be at peace for years, and I was so grateful that it did happen, and certainly in a way that could not be denied.

I wrote a letter to the family members about a week later and recounted what took place and the time. I got a call from Damien's parents, and each of them thanked me and said it gave them comfort. Angels work in ways that we can recognize if we allow ourselves to pay attention and acknowledge them.

Angels Around Us

Angels have a way of letting us know that they are always around us. I usually tell people to pray, and your angel will surely guide you.

Another friend of ours, Edith, is a prayerful person who attends mass at least twice a week. She joyfully drives the five miles to church with her friend Loretta, and then they go out for lunch.

On a very cold December day, the ladies noticed a couple walking briskly down the sidewalk. Their clothing seemed to be very worn and tattered. When Edith and Loretta arrived at the church, they noticed these same people in the distance. Edith wanted to talk with them, but Loretta had an appointment that afternoon and was in a hurry, so they were unable to talk to the couple.

The following week, Edith noticed these same people walking along the sidewalk and inside the church. Edith told Loretta that she wanted to talk with them. Perhaps they could use a ride or something. Loretta was hesitant because she didn't know them. No one seemed to be approaching them, and Edith wanted to take the initiative.

Edith went up to the woman and introduced herself. The woman in the tattered winter coat said, "Hello, my name is Mary." Edith noticed that the man had gotten up to go to the back of the church by the men's room.

Edith asked Mary if she could help and if she was new to the area. Mary said, "Yes, we are new, but we like to walk and can manage." Edith invited Mary and her husband to lunch, but Mary declined. Edith said, "I will be here again next Wednesday. Perhaps you will change your mind and I can assist you because it is so cold outside." Mary said, "Thank you so much for your kindness. Joseph and I will take that into consideration. We will go now." Edith walked toward the back of the church, with Loretta looking on, and had an incredible happy feeling.

The following week, Edith and Loretta did not notice the people walking on the sidewalk, nor were they in church. Edith remembers the warm feeling that she had after she spoke with Mary. She realized that they had to be angels and were there to see what person would show that simple act of kindness. Edith did exactly that. It was only after the fact that Edith realized that she was indeed in the presence of an angel or angels.

Edith and I spoke after her experience, and since it was during the Christmas season, we thought it might even be the real Mary and Joseph visiting to see who would assist them. We both laughed and I said, "Well, we will have to wait and see until we get to heaven who your visitors really were. Only the Lord can tell us exactly." We agreed and thought it was indeed a very special and unique experience.

Angels Live in the Unseen—
Unless Permitted to be Seen

Angels also can prevent you from harm. When Maudy and I first met, I told her about a time I felt an angel was involved. I wanted to know if my suspicion was correct.

I was on my way to work in downtown Charlotte and my mind was preoccupied with a difficult family situation. I was approaching an intersection and thought the light was green. I went through the light and felt the cars hitting my car. Everyone was blowing their horns. Within a few seconds, I knew something was wrong—why weren't these people stopping? I felt as if an invisible hand was pushing my car to the right-hand side of the road.

It still did not dawn on me why these drivers could not see that they were hitting my car and in the wrong. Everything seemed to be in slow motion. People were still blowing their horns, and after I was pushed out of the intersection, I parked on the side of the road. I was shaking uncontrollably from head to toe and thought, "What are these crazy drivers doing?" Then it set in. I was the one who went through the red light without one dent to my car, and that invisible hand was an angel saving my life.

Saving Angel in Times of Distress

Angels certainly do make themselves heard in times of difficulty, and sometimes people hear audible messages. Maudy and I met a woman named Patricia who was particularly

concerned about Ann, her teenage daughter. Ann was living on her own and involved with someone that Patricia
did not particularly like. With her own motherly intuition,
Patricia suspected that Ann was in an abusive relationship.

With a heavy heart, Patricia kept praying. One day after
she spoke with Ann, her suspicion was confirmed. This man
had been taking money from Ann and physically assaulted
her a few times.

This message, although good to know, doesn't give you
comfort when you know your daughter is still there. Ann
said she was going to devise a plan to run away from this
man and that she would not talk to Patricia for a month or
so because she did not want to endanger her mother's life.
Patricia was very worried, but she knew that Ann was a
good woman and would be able to do this.

One day while taking a nap, Patricia heard an audible
message: "I will rescue her." The word "rescue" denotes dan-
ger, so Patricia knew that this must have been an angelic
message to put her mind at ease about her daughter.

Within a month of this message, Patricia received a
call from Ann. She was with friends in another state, and
the man who had been abusing her was entangled with
other police problems and an arrest was imminent.

Angels come to assist in whatever way necessary, and
they are placed in our path by heaven to see how we will
handle particular situations. They are always around us. All
we need to do is pray and you will recognize them.

On Angels Wings

The previous beautiful angel section was primarily written by Gail. I wanted you all to know that angels are truly right beside us all the time. It is a powerful message of recognizing God's angels who sometimes appear in human form as the strangers who help us throughout life. In times of distress, illness, trouble, or any crisis, please call upon the angels. Your prayers will be answered.

Since angels are so important, we don't want you to miss their presence or the messages they pass along to you. They are the links between the loved ones in heaven and people here on earth and can work in the seen and unseen. Angels can communicate through a song. For example, when you turn on the radio and hear exactly the song you wanted to hear. It may remind you of someone who has passed or was a favorite of theirs while here on earth. Angels can also produce a scent, like the scent of roses, as it might have been their favorite flower while on earth and a sign you would recognize from your loved one who has passed.

Angels are pure positive energy and relay life-affirming messages. They can't wait to let you know the good news they bring and are there to let your inner voice speak to you. Angels are messengers. They have no free will and don't have opinions. They whisper suggestions or instructions or create in your mind's eye an image that they want you to see.

Don't be disappointed if they resist appearing to you. There is a saying, "To sense the presence of an angel is like feeling the wind all around you. You cannot actually see the wind, but you can notice its movement and you know it is there." If there is positive human action taking place, then angels do not need to give assistance. People are disappointed when they do not see things the way they want to see them. We must learn that heaven gives us what we need at a particular point in life.

Guardian Angels

Guardian angels are exactly what the name indicates. They guard, guide, protect, and illuminate our path of life. They are appointed by a heavenly counsel and approved by God especially for you. Guardian angels will lead you to places they know you need to go and push you to do things they know it is time for you to do. They work with you and for you. Through prayer and meditation, you can dial into your personal guardian angels and establish direct communication. If you embrace the seven elements and are positive, make changes, and have faith, you may be able to see and hear the angels that are always around to guide and protect you and keep you out of trouble.

Dreams

We all dream every night, even if sometimes we cannot remember what happens after we wake up. Dreams can carry thoughts, images, or emotions during our sleep. We might be asleep, but our subconscious mind keeps going. Dreams are direct messages and a preview of your life.

Although dreams are cryptic, they are my language. It is very simple for me to explain dreams. Our loved ones in heaven do not speak the human language anymore. When we cross over, we speak from thought to thought or mind to mind as in telepathy.

Sometimes we get irritated because we want to remember our dreams, but can't. The way to retrieve these dream-lost moments is to let it go for the time being. Once you let go, the memory starts coming back through flashes. These flashes could be in a conversation with people or visualizing something in your mind through the experiences of the day.

Then the "Aha" moments will come back, as in "Oh, yes. That's what the dream was about." It's like putting the dream-puzzle together to get the full picture. Like so many things in life, by letting go of it, you will let it come back to you.

Keep a dream journal beside your bed, and as soon as you wake up, write down what happens and date it. After you write down the events of your dream, you analyze it and refer back to your dream journal to see if the dreams come to pass. It's pretty interesting how you get to know more about how heaven communicates with you.

Prepare, Prevent, Provide

Messages are carried through dreams to prepare, prevent, or provide. For example, if you have a dream about water, that means trouble. Your dream is telling you to beware in order to prevent, avoid, or prepare you for a certain situation.

Olive shared a recurrent dream with me. It was about a very large bumblebee that kept bothering her. It would hover over her, then explode, and a large amount of water would splash down onto her. To me, the meaning was very clear. A busybody in her workplace was giving her problems, and she had not fully addressed the matter. Olive agreed, and I told her that she would conquer the situation.

Our dreams are also portals for our loved ones to communicate with us. When you wake up and can't remember your dream, but are left with a good feeling and wonder why you feel the way you do, you have been visiting with your family or friends in heaven. Your deceased loved ones can't come back to stay, but they are allowed to visit and check in with us.

When you dream about your loved ones, wake up feeling positive, and are able to remember the dream in vivid color, this means something good is about to happen in your life. The message your loved ones are sending is: "You are being provided for and taken care of."

People often ask: "Why don't my parents come into my dreams?" If this occurs, it is because your emotions are in the way. Stress and anxiety subconsciously block our loved ones from access to our dreams. The reason most often is that we cannot let go of our loved ones who have passed and we continue to live in depression. In order to have this veil lifted, we need to embrace love and reverse our depression. Everyone in heaven lives in love, truth, and revelation. The only way our relatives can contact us is through love. Then, the person who has passed is able to do earthly work from heaven to help loved ones left behind so they can do heavenly work here on earth.

When you are relaxed and calm, you leave your dream door open and your loved ones can visit with you. When you control your mind, you will control your life and keep your portal open for heavenly visitors.

Dreams Believed Are Dreams Achieved

Sometimes people will say, "Maudy, I had an awful dream. What does that mean?" I explain that there are many reasons. Problems you don't want to deal with by day can creep into your mind subconsciously at night. Perhaps you need to deal with a problematic situation that has caused you mental stress. This obviously will cause fear or insecurity. When a dream is explained to me in detail, I will be able to clarify this. When I tap into the vibration of your voice, it will be visible for me.

Here's an example. Jack and Anne lost their daughter Jessica to suicide. Jack had a dream about going to a wedding in Charleston, South Carolina, and his other daughter Jennifer was walking next to him. Jack had an empty wheelchair and was looking for Jessica to see if he could help her. In the distance, he could see this bright white bridge crossing the river but was horrified to see that people were jumping off the bridge.

I immediately understood Jessica's message. She is now okay and was asking her parents to assist people who were near suicide. He got very emotional and said Jessica's friends had already been to see him and his wife. He said they'd assisted them with their grief and would continue to do so. Even though Jack was concerned about his dream, it had a positive message of love and hope to go forward.

Jessica was doing earthly work from heaven by sending friends to her parents for emotional support. It was difficult but also soothing to the parents because their child is truly alive in spirit to them.

My Dream

I used to be a dental assistant, and in my dream I was visiting the dentist that I used to work for in Holland. He passed a few years ago. This dream was very brief and the only thing I remember saying was "Hey, Doctor. What are you doing here? Shouldn't you be ..." Then I woke up.

About two months after this dream, I had a dental appointment to have a tooth filled. I had this done many times before, so it was no big deal. The doctor usually gives me gas to relax before injecting novocaine into my gum. I have never had problems with this physically.

When I was given the anesthesia, I started to connect with family members of the doctor and dental assistant who were working on me. Then I fell into a deep sleep and I could hear things but they sounded far away, like I was there, but not.

Suddenly I heard a woman saying, "My dear, will you tell Harold that I am here, and also tell him Paul, Robert, and Henry are here too!" I heard myself saying, as I always do when I deliver messages, "Yes, ma'am. I will!" Then I said, "Who can I say is calling?" I heard her laughing and she said, "Oh, I am a newcomer. My name is Margaret."

Apparently I was telling the dentist all of this while I was under in this deep sleep. He knows of my gift and is intrigued. Margaret was giving me all of this information. Then I heard someone in the room ask about my cell phone. By this time, I felt somewhat awkward and had heaviness in my head because of the anesthetic. I thought, "I am on the phone. Why do you need my cell phone for?" I heard myself saying, "Just call Gail. She knows!"

By this time Margaret was back and said, "They can't hear you, my dear. No one can hear you. Only us!" I was very confused and had no idea why I was so disconnected.

Then I saw many people and heard an ambulance siren. I thought someone must be in an accident. That someone was me! I wasn't in an accident, I just couldn't wake up. On the way to the emergency room, a med-tech in the ambulance called Gail and my husband and family to notify them that I was headed to the hospital. Gail thought it had to be a mistake. I had gone to a dentist appointment.

Once I was at the hospital, I went through the whole nine yards of tests. The doctors finally discovered I had dangerously low potassium, which caused me to go into a deep sleep. The doctors said that if I had not had this dental appointment, I could have been taking a nap or going to bed at night and never have woken up.

I called the dentist to apologize. I felt very bad for what I'd put him and his staff through. He couldn't have possibly known my condition, and I didn't have a clue. The dentist was so nice and very concerned about me not gaining consciousness and said, "Maudy, you mentioned Margaret in the conversation. At the time, I had no idea who you were talking about. However, a few days later, I received an obituary in the mail from a relative that my Great-Aunt Margaret passed away. In fact, she passed the same day you were here! You also mentioned Robert and that's my father. Paul is my uncle and Henry is my grandfather. This is really unbelievable!" I thought to myself, "Yes, tell me about it!"

Understanding the Dream

My preview was my dream about the dentist I used to work for. The feeling that I was there, but not, speaks for itself. I was there and no one could hear me.

This potassium situation was a health issue and seemed to be a silent killer. I did not know I had this deficiency as I am under the care of a physician and go for regular check-ups. The instructions were very clear: I have a mission to fulfill and I need to pay attention to my health and get everything under control.

Heaven certainly has a funny way of letting me pay attention. Letting me go through this frightening experience was necesary to bring long-term health to my attention, which is necessary for me to fulfill my mission. It might not be the way we like it, but it is the way it needs to be handled.

When we "let go and let God," we skip the panic route and let Him lead the way. When duty calls, I need to be in good shape and healthy with these silent obstacles out of my way.

Daydreams

Daydreams are wishful creations of our imagination. They are more powerful than you might expect because they are the goals or desires that a person sets in their mind. Your thoughts can take you to a platform where you are able to have a visual of your wishful creation. Daydreams can turn into night dreams and thus be answered. If you have daydreamed about a particular situation for a long time, when you have a night dream about it, you could have your answer.

Daydreams can start consciously as being aware of the wish, desire, and will to take the mind into the subconscious thinking part. It is best to daydream on your own time, in private, and in silence. Have a prayer attached to this special time and you will have heaven's assistance to let the angels process your daydream.

Visions

Visions are supernatural appearances received through eyesight that reveal an event in the past or future. It is also a direct mystical awareness of the supernatural in visible form. In other words, you might see someone who has passed only for a split second. You might even be able to describe what they were wearing. Supernaturally gifted people are more in tune with the second type of vision (which everyone has on some level). They are able to clarify and recognize this manifestation. in the split second it is present and then describe what you have seen in detail.

Visions can be messages for missions. Everyone is gifted and we all have powerful intuition, feelings, and senses that you can tap into and be able to receive visions. It is a beautiful ability and will happen when it is meant to assist you along life's journey.

Supernatural Ability

People often ask me: "Maudy, how do I get what you have?" I smile and tell them to listen, live, and learn. Most of all, I explain that it takes a lot of personal sacrifice to be in complete submission to the will of God. All it takes is prayer for a deeper faith and trust. Ask heaven to have God increase your gifts. When you let it come, you will let it go as well. Gail tells people, "Pray before you wish for something like this. There is a very big sacrifice and this gift is never for personal gain, only for those that have been placed upon your path."

In presentations I explain that I only want to inspire you to be a difference by making a difference. I also tell people that I am able to give assistance, but I don't solve your problems. You are in charge of your own life and what you do with it. Your visions are your mission.

Angel Whispers
We are all documented in Heaven's Archives
Heaven is observing our earthly lives
Heavenly Angels are here, there and everywhere
Everyday and every night they guide and give light
Angels work through people as the 'stranger' with
the heart of gold
With their arms to hold—you
It's what they do
Angels have no free will or opinion, they simply act
As a matter of fact
Angels come when you pray
Angels lead the way
And
Are there at no cost when you're . . . lost

On Belief: Maudisms to Remember

A Maudism (or Coat Hanger) is a phrase to memorize and remember to hang on to when you are facing difficult situations.

To Believe Is to Achieve and to Receive

....

Belief is having Faith

....

Faith doesn't have any doubt ... Faith has no fear

....

To Believe is to see

....

*Once you believe in yourself, you will believe
   in your higher power*

....

*To Sense the Presence of an Angel ... is like feeling
   the wind all around you*

....

Dreams—prepare—prevent—provide

....

Dreams Believed are Dreams Achieved

....

Your Visions are your Mission

CONCLUSION

The Seven Elements Change Lives

The seven elements of the spiritual law will indeed change your life. Each one of us has at least one that we need to work on within our lives. As you have seen by each story that illustrates a particular element, people need to work on their own element and get past the block that has prevented them from having a better life. Life is to be enjoyed and now is the time for you.

These seven elements are the constant thread within this book that will enable you to restructure your life brick by brick. Life is a constant learning experience and we encourage you to enjoy this book and your new life that will emerge.

The valuable information within these powerful stories has no price tag and is only to treasure. When the heavy luggage from the past disappears, your life's journey slowly becomes featherlight and your path will be illuminated.

The way to maintain this is to practice these elements faithfully within your daily life. Each one of you has a particular element you have to work on. Once you decide which element needs work, simply home in on it and work on it until it becomes embedded within your life. It is all about practice, practice, practice.

Preview for Life

Previews of life have been shown to you throughout your own life's experiences. These previews have prepared you for what is coming down the road. All of life's lessons are to teach you how to understand and handle you.

Through my own life experiences, I had to recognize where I needed to be. I needed to understand myself and my preview for my life.

You also need to recognize these life previews in your own life. We often don't, can't, or won't pay attention because of our emotions and life difficulties. Dreams can also be previews of what is coming, as detailed in the previous chapter.

Previews can be an experience you need to go through to prepare and strengthen you so you are able to act and react when necessary. I'm sure many of you have had previews of life. Maybe it manifested as a strange feeling or dreams that were too cryptic to understand. When we reflect on the preview, we might recognize what it was trying to tell us. Learn to see and recognize your life preview. Ask yourself and review where you were in the past? What and who crossed your path? Once you review your list, you will see where you are today and you can answer the question "Why?"

How to Identify Life Previews

Perhaps when you were a child you played "school" all the time with your siblings and friends. Then, as you grew, you felt that you really enjoyed it and decided to become a teacher. This a preview.

Then you start college. You decide to get married while in school and had an unexpected surprise—you got pregnant. Did that preview end? Of course not. You simply took a temporary detour. The finances were not there once the child arrived and studying became difficult. However, as the child grew, you realized, "I can do this again." So you resume your life preview and get your teaching degree.

The desire to be a teacher started at age five or six, and it remained until you and life were ready to continue. Your preview can be almost anything. Think back to your childhood. What did you say as a child? "When I grow up I want to be ..." What prepared you for today? Things become clear, which is a beautiful thing. It's very cool once you increase your perception and learn to see your previews.

The Artist Within

Gail's dad worked in a paper mill, so there were always paper and crayons around the house. She started to draw in kindergarten. Even though Gail worked in the business world, art was a thread through her entire career and a preview for Gail in many aspects of her life. She produces videos, is an avid photographer, and now paints and exhibits her art.

In order to see things clearly, you need to open your heart and your mind to help you grow. As your ability to recognize previews becomes stronger, your awareness becomes more spiritual and maintain peace with a clear mind.

Radio Call-In

Sometimes life previews can take place as a tremendous hardship, as evidenced by Amanda. Our original contact with Amanda came as a result of her calling in to a local radio show where Gail and I were studio guests. The phone lines at the radio station were completely lit up, and Amanda stayed on the line for about thirty minutes before we could get to her.

Amanda felt pushed by something or someone to call. This was indeed an angel push. Nothing is ever a coincidence. She explained she would ordinarily never seek paranormal advice but had been depressed about a situation and needed some assistance. She asked, "Maudy, why do I feel like there is a void in my life? I feel so empty." I asked her, "Amanda, who is Carol?" Amanda was in shock and answered, "My father passed away and we just found out that my father's name on the birth certificate was not Carl, but Carol!" Because this was acknowledged, I heard even more heavenly information and asked if she could call Gail and we'd set up a phone appointment so I could tell her more.

When that phone contact was made, we got to the bottom of her situation. Amanda and her mom were sick at the same time and took care of each other during their illnesses. Her sister was also ill. Amanda's mom lost her battle with cancer and Amanda had to go to the hospital for an exploratory heart surgery. I also found out that Amanda's dad had passed a few months before her mom and sister were diagnosed with cancer. It was lot to deal with all at once.

Amanda shared with me that she knew something was going to happen. She had flashes of seeing everything white and she didn't understand why. When she was telling me her story, it was as if my heart stopped beating. However, it was not my heart, it was Amanda's!

During Amanda's exploratory heart surgery, the surgeon accidentally cut Amanda's aorta, causing Amanda to flatline—she was clinically dead for a few minutes. Amanda woke up after the surgery only to realize that it was five days later. She had been in a coma.

The explanation of Amanda's flashes of seeing everything white is that when Amanda died for a few minutes and slipped into a coma, she was on the white plane, which is between heaven and earth. This white plane was to allow her to be in touch with herself and a comfortable preview place of Amanda's life.

It was not Amanda's time to be in heaven. She had a near-death experience as a different way to help prepare her to continue her mission here on earth. Amanda may never know exactly what happened during those five days, but she will get flashbacks that will help her go forward.

This is all positive and is between the soul and God. This did cause the void that Amanda experienced because she lost five days. Because of this void, she became depressed.

The moral of Amanda's ordeal is that her heart was broken long before the surgeon cut her aorta. However, Amanda needed to look at her heart because of the many things in her personal life that had hurt her and caused her depression. Many of those things had cut her to the core, and now she had to reevaluate the depression that came into her life. It was there before and now she had to work to restructure her life and eliminate the sadness within her mind that caused her life heartache.

Amanda had lost her father, mother, and sister, and all within two years. And she almost died herself. Now she was given a second chance to change and finish the mission. Her father had approval from heaven to comfort her and confirm many of Amanda's thoughts. Heaven works in mysterious but miraculous and magical ways.

This preview for Amanda's scenario can only be recognized after the fact. It was a preparation for what was about to happen. Amanda actually experienced her preview in a safe time to rejuvenate her spirit. Use these heavenly words as a reminder, "Something is about to happen. Just inhale and exhale and all will be well. We'll do the rest!"

Attain, Retain, and Maintain = Strong ARM

Have you ever had a moment when you have either physically or mentally had the wind knocked out of you? If so, this section will help you attain strength, retain courage, and maintain your willpower.

I explain that in times of distress, hardship, and crisis, you need to feel the arms of an angel embracing you. That's because during these stressful times, we find it difficult to stay strong. The nagging "Why?" questions arise and you wonder, "What should I do next?"

I grew up in a small farmers' village in Holland and was a chiropodist/pedicurist. I used to visit the farmers out in the country and treat their feet because they wore wooden shoes.

Mr. Willem was one of these farmers, and I always enjoyed his wisdom and his way of speaking. On a particular visit he said, "Maudy, do you know why we have to forgive our enemies?" He caught me off guard and I said, "Yes, because God wants us to!" He smiled and said, "I am sure that is what God wants! But we have to forgive our enemies because it messes up their heads!" At first I thought it was a strange statement. Then I got exactly what he was trying to say—that forgiving our enemies makes them think about their actions—and started to laugh.

Mr. Willem had incredible wisdom, and to this day I remember a lot of things that he told me. One of his phrases that I really like is, "Keep your fences horse-high, pig-tight, and bull-strong!"

Many nights when I would come home I'd think about this phrase and make a note to myself to attain, retain, and maintain in times of distress—and to pass this on to others. It's not what you learn in life, it's how you learn to live with what you've learned. This was all part of what helped me build up strength. As a result of these farmers like Mr. Willem, I learned to look at my strength and never the weakness.

Keeping the fences horse-high, pig-tight, and bull-strong is self-protection when life happens. We cannot fulfill our mission when we are vulnerable. We all try to put up a front; however, it will catch up with us sooner or later. When we don't face what we need to face, it will also affect the people around us. This happened to someone I met along the way. I felt driven to bring purpose with a strong arm to his attention.

Dodging the Bullet

I had to attend an important business meeting by myself. Gail usually accompanies me when I travel, but this time I needed to go alone. Gail is aware that I always get side-tracked with people, especially strangers who are not a stranger to me. I always forget that I should not get into their business, especially when they start to talk to me.

I was at the Charlotte airport, waiting to board my flight to Tampa, Florida, when a man across from me started to talk in Spanish. I explained that I don't speak Spanish, I'm from Holland, and my parents came from the islands of New Guinea. The man introduced himself as Christopher and told me he was on his way to Texas for the funeral of his uncle, who was shot to death. I expressed my condolences and told him I would pray for him and his family. Christopher asked if I would mind if he sat next to me so he could hear me better. While he was switching places, I heard the sharp soaring and squeaking sound of a bullet. He told me, "You mentioned prayer. I wish I knew more. I just don't know what or how to pray. I just can't find the right words." I smiled at him and said, "Christopher, just because the right words do not come does not mean the prayer is not prayed!"

Then he said, "I have so many setbacks in life. I'm becoming bitter and resentful to a point that I am falling into depression. I really don't know why I am even telling you all of this." I smiled and responded, "Setbacks happen to give you a chance and a choice for you to move forward." I felt pushed to open a different conversation.

Before I changed the conversation completely, I asked if he believed in angels. His answer was "Of course, who doesn't? It's just sometimes I wonder if they ever come around me." I explained that I am able to listen to angel whispers. Christopher smiled and looked at me with the "Yeah, whatever" eyes.

He then said, "Where are the angels when you need them?" I immediately responded by saying, "There are many angels. And besides, how many angels does it take to change a light bulb?" I had to break the ice, and he laughed out loud. Now was the time to address the information I had received.

I asked Christopher what he was doing with children. He smiled and told me that he was a youth counselor. He also told me that he had been in the army and served in Iraq for a year prior to becoming a counselor. Then I felt the strict and stern feeling inside of me, which is what I refer to calling him to the order.

I said, "Christopher, it was not your fault. It's time to let go!" He immediately became defensive and asked me, "Why did you say that and what do you know?" My thoughts were, "Good. You asked for the light, and the light 'we' will certainly give you!" Then I asked, "Who is Brian?" Now he had a look of disbelief on his face and was in shock when he heard this name. He explained that Brian was a friend who was killed in Iraq six months before Christopher was deployed. Then I asked, "Who is Ryan?"

By this time, Christopher became very emotional and had buried his head in his hands and started to cry. He said, "Who are you, and why are you bringing this up? It should have been me. Why wasn't it me?"

Now the door had been opened and I told him, "It was Brian who pushed you down, and you dodged the bullet!" As Christopher was stuttering and trying to get the words out, he started to say, "You don't understand I dropped…" He couldn't finish the sentence. I finished it for him by saying, "You dropped your magazine and your rifle. Wasn't it an M-16? The bullet hit your friend Ryan and killed him instantly. Now you walk around mad and still feel guilty and ask yourself 'Why not me?'"

When that strict and stern feeling remains, I usually continue addressing the person in front of me. I told him, "Christopher, what don't you understand? It was not your time! You dropped all of your stuff because Brian pushed you down. Brian had orders from higher up to do earthly work from heaven and had to pick up your friend Ryan, not you!"

I continued so he would fully understand. "You need to fulfill your mission here on earth. Your mission is to help the children do heavenly work here on earth! How can you help the children when you can't help yourself to make peace with you?" I explained to Christopher that from heaven's point of view, there is no blame or guilt, only experience in how you handle what has happened to you. Further, I told him he became his own enemy by creating all negative thoughts. Now he had to learn to forgive himself especially for being negative toward himself.

By this time, Christopher put his arms around me. I felt his tears, and I could hardly breathe because he was holding me so tight. I told him, "Accept the help from your friend in heaven so you can help God's children. Let go and honor the past, as the past is honoring you. You are here for your own purpose, goal, and destiny. You are still in the service, remember?" Finally he became calmer and composed himself. He smiled at me and said, "You know what? You are actually a total stranger to me!" I responded by saying, "You know what? My friend Gail was concerned and advised me not to talk to strangers. However, my heavenly orders were that you had to hear it from a stranger."

Then he said, "Maudy, I am going to ask if I can sit next to you on the plane. I have so much to ask you. It's so nice that we are traveling together!" Then I had to break the news to him and said, "I am sorry, but we are not traveling together. This is not your gate!" He said, "What do you mean?" I said, "Look at your ticket. You have a different gate number. You better go now because your plane is boarding at this moment! You will make it. Go ahead."

It was amusing to see the surprise on his face. He said, "How did this happen and why did this happen?" I smiled and said, "Here we go again. Questioning life and accepting life. Life happens! It was nice meeting you. Just for the record, the light bulb is changed!" All of the burdensome emotions seemed to have disappeared and replaced by relief, joy, and laughter. This is the way it has to be when the lights are turned on again.

By this time, it was time for me to board my plane. It's so cool for me to see people go into this positive shock mode and watch the healing process at the same time.

What I want to emphasize to you about this particular scenario is that whatever the destination in life, it's not what happens to you, but how you handle what happens to you! Christopher was put on my path, because "we"— me and his friends from heaven—wanted to free him from the guilt-luggage he was holding onto. The thought came back into my head about Mr. Willem and his funny saying about forgiving enemies and how it messes up their heads. In Christopher's case, his head was already messed up before he met us. His friends from heaven and

I had to show him how to forgive himself, and it was to undo what he had created for himself. Sometimes things get worse before they get better. To me, this is a proven fact to understand heaven's way of dealing with life and its obstacles. In this case, the obstacle was the "why" questions he could not let go of.

Holding on to the past and not letting go will make and keep you a prisoner of your own life. What you are doing is allowing yourself to be the keepsake of your past. You will not be able to live life but life will be living you. Feel the arms of an angel around you and learn to hold on to where the angel holds on to you!

Live Life to the Fullest

Through the angels' grapevine, you have been given a little glimpse of heaven here on earth. As you now know, everything is recorded and reported in heaven, and all of your prayers are received. What you do in the dark will always come out in the light.

To live life to the fullest, you must be kind to your mind. The mind has a powerful energy; it can make or break you. To master your mind is to master your life.

It takes courage to step up to our own plate. The simplest way to remember this is CCC, which means control, charge, choice. When you recognize your thoughts, you will be able to recognize yourself. The CCC will give you the ability to eventually let you see the world from a healthier and happier point of view.

To take charge with control and choice is to stay focused upon yourself with love, honor, and respect. As you recognize in your own journey, it is too easy to let people around you take control away from you. Allows things to happen *to us* is what causes stress, frustration, and depression. When things work against us mentally, it will usually show physically.

Staying in control also means closing the door to the past real fast. In other words, you must let go of the familiar old luggage. Only when we close the door from the past will we be able to make room for the future.

Keep Dancing

This section is dedicated to people who have experienced illnesses. You will see how even in these difficult circumstances, you can live life to the fullest.

This story is about a man who is very special to me and whom I greatly admire. Rudolph has strengthened my own faith, respect, and courage. He has endured cancer with being upbeat, optimistic, and courageous. For those of you going through a similar experience, I want to share this man's outlook on life. I also want to bring his wife to your attention. As the caregiver, she had a strong role in supporting and taking care of her husband.

For many years before Rudolph was diagnosed, he and his wife had a great passion for ballroom dancing. They danced a couple of times a week and enjoyed it very much. When Rudolph was undergoing chemo treatments, he and his wife kept dancing. I had great admiration in how strong and upbeat he was during these times. When I spoke to him on the phone, we often talked about how many treatments he still had to face.

When I asked Rudolph how he was doing, I was always surprised by his answer. He said, "Oh, Maudy, you have to keep dancing and stay positive. Yes, of course, the chemo treatment makes me tired and sick, but then I'll rest and give myself time to regain strength. It doesn't help to get depressed even though I am facing uncertainty of my illness. You just have to fight and conquer."

His determined words were so powerful that I could recognize the strength in healing. Because his wife was a great support for him in their life challenge, the endurance process maintained to be positive.

Through conversations with his wife, I saw how she as caregiver was coping with the care of her husband. Of course, it was very hard for her to see her husband go through this painful time. I could see how both Rudolph and his wife were using their courage in a very special way.

When challenged with a disease, the focus is usually on the person going through the disease and the caregiver of the patient is often overlooked. However, it is wise for all of you who are in the position of caregiver to make sure you take a little time for you.

Rudolph decided to live life to the fullest. He is now cancer free and decided to take a vacation with his wife to Arizona to visit with his daughter, her husband, and his first grandchild. His willpower, love, honor, and respect helped him mentally and physically get through this difficult time. The care and support from his wife, family, friends, and the medical world was an important factor for his healing. He discovered that willpower is the mother of courage and love for yourself.

The cancer stayed in remission for about six months, and Rudolph had made the most of it. He continued to dance and enjoy his family members, taking several international trips to do so. But the illness came back.

During this special time of embracing life, Rudolph decided to take his wife dancing for one last dance. It was after one of these sessions that Rudolph passed quietly and was called home to heaven. I want to point out that sometimes a remission becomes a heavenly understanding of being in remission.

For Rudolph, this means he was qualified and promoted from a successfully lived life to now doing earthly work from heaven as he did his heavenly work here.

Fight and Conquer

In Rudolph's situation, a key element was the strong factor of love. It takes faith and trust in each other. It is of the highest importance to believe in yourself and the power of prayer. In all experiences of disease and illnesses, the power of prayer will show you miracles with the grace of God to grant us the time to fulfill the mission. My prayers are with you who are still facing these difficult times. I hope this story gave you a light to guide.

Many people experience the negative aspects of these scenarios which often can mentally damage and decrease the recovery process. Rudolph brought the message to never allow yourself to have self-pity. If you go down this path, it will open a door straight to depression. We have to strengthen our faith and belief to conquer insecurity. The question many people ask is: "How do you do that when facing or going through such a difficult situation?" Let's take you further to help you to the answer as a choice to look into.

Think Positive

Everything starts with the powerful energy of your mind. In many situations, our emotions get in the way. When we think positive, it will automatically escalate into positive energy. Positive attracts positive!

In many ways, positive thinking will provide strength and it is a great platform for you to start with love for you. Standing on this platform, you will notice that you develop self-confidence to conquer fear and overcome life challenges. Many people say; "Yes, Maudy, that's easy to say but that's not for everyone."

My answer is we all have a choice. The choice is to make positive decisions—and that starts with willpower. When life works against us, you can make this positive choice that leads to finding the courage to get up and do something about it.

Make the choice to live with love for you. Learning to adapt to positive habits and live it consciously means accepting life through self-realization.

Look at Your Strength, not the Weakness
Maybe you have recognized yourselves in one of these scenarios. Hopefully it will give you an insight and help you with your life's process. Through this different out-look of life, we can come to a point where we understand what we need to learn when facing hardship and experiencing illness. It is in these difficult times when we have to look at our strengths, not our weaknesses.

It is important to take one day at a time and learn to live in today. We can open the door of courage for you, but it takes you to go through this door. With willpower, love, and faith, we can conquer ourselves, whereby we will be able to make different life choices.

Each and every life experience does indeed build you up. The life in which we live is a never-ending learning process. Learning does not stop when we leave our family home or college. We are never too old to learn. So next time, someone tells you they are "too old to learn," encourage them to believe that we are constantly learning, and age is never a barrier.

Through Thick and Thin

Going through the experience of illness can bring people closer or cause them to drift apart. In situations described in this story, heaven observes the people who stand tall with love and the people who walked away from love.

There's a phrase: "You can count the people on one hand who are actually there for you." When we are ambushed by illness, the illness can be a mission or a challenge. If it is a mission, the people going through the illness have a chance to overcome this. One can be a survivor to make the choice to assist others in and on their journey to provide encouragement and empowerment. I always remind people "to live with expectations is to live with disappointments."

When there is a challenge involved, we might be asked to look into the seven elements. When you come to understand this concept, you will learn to see above and beyond. Remember, it's not what you look at that matters, it is what you see.

It is beautiful to see how heaven will put people on linked paths with similar illness experiences to help you on the way. You will also recognize the people who are the survivors and serve the mission by publicly speaking up or building foundations and starting organizations. The mission of being a survivor is to pass on assistance by paying it forward and helping others who are in need.

Through our life experiences, we are confronted to overcome ourselves first before helping others to overcome. It's a "heavenly observed" part of our life training.

You Are a Student of Your Own Life Experience

Our life experience is our life training; therefore, we are a student from our own life experience. We can only become a teacher when we've overcome ourselves and learn to live the intangible gifts. When God places people in front me, it is my mission to answer their questions and bring cause and effect to the attention. In my world, it takes a stranger to give the light when you're lost. When we learn, we teach. When we teach we continue to learn.

Even though it's hard to stay upbeat in difficult times, we can make the choice to look at what we can do and look at what we have and who we are.

This book is based upon a moral. What is the moral of your story? Each and every one of us has a story and a journey we are traveling. Look at the situation you are facing and analyze the moral of the story. When doing this, ask yourself the following questions:

What did I learn from this? How can I pay it forward?

How could I have changed to accomplish a better outcome?

When am I ready to change?

Why was I placed upon this particular path?

What can I do to make my life better?

One thing to remember is that it begins with you first. Once you examine your own conscience to see what could have been done better, you will make changes—if you want to.

The end of this book is the beginning of your life story. We hope that you create your own life story with the information provided in this book.

Love, blessings and prayers,

Maudy and Gail

Accept and Let Go
Closer to the clue, as we reach that part of life
We realize how important it is,
The way we survive
Nothing is yours, Nothing is mine
We are only here to take care and to share as
We fly in time
Something special can be taken away
From you and me—

Not able to realize, blind to see
So we fly in time, closer to the clue
To carry on doing the things that we do
Not to ask ourselves why,
For there will be no answer,
But to fly on the wings of time.
Fly through sun, fly through rain,
Fly through "Why questions,"
Fly through life's pain.
Stronger we become—If we want to
Survivors in Happiness—If we let it,
Because once we reach that part of life,
It will let us know
That life's clue is: How to Accept and Let Go

THE
ANGEL
CODE

*Your Interactive Guide
to Angelic Communication*

CHANTEL LYSETTE

The Angel Code
Your Interactive Guide to Angelic Communication
CHANTEL LYSETTE

Is that song on the radio a sign from heaven?

With signature sass and wit, Chantel Lysette offers a fun, hands-on program for getting in touch with your angels. She'll help you sharpen your intuitive skills, create an ideal meditation space, and open yourself to divine guidance. Get acquainted with sixteen different angels—their personalities, the feelings they evoke, how they may appear, numerous associations, and countless other clues for recognizing their presence and deciphering angelic messages. Worksheets and journal pages allow you to easily record your spiritual encounters and compile your own unique "angel code" for connecting with Gabriel, Metatron, Michael, Raphael, and other heavenly hosts.

978-0-7387-2123-1, 288 pp., 7½ x 9⅛   **$17.95**

ENHANCE RELATIONSHIPS WITH YOUR SPIRITUAL COMPANIONS

GUIDES
guardians
AND
angels

D.J. CONWAY

Guides, Guardians and Angels
Enhance Relationships with Your Spiritual Companions
D. J. CONWAY

We may not see them. We may not hear them. But angels and spirit guides are with us all the time. Who are these entities? What is their purpose? How can we communicate with them?

Guides, Guardians and Angels is much more than an in-depth, cross-cultural exploration of these otherworldly beings. D. J. Conway reveals the role of these spiritual companions play and demonstrates how to develop a relationship with them through meditation, chants, rituals, and spells.

Take a fascinating tour of the multilayered Otherworld. Catch a glimpse of life between lives. Discover how power animals, nature spirits, dragons, light and shadow angels, and the spirits of friends, family, and pets fit into the spiritual equation. Revolutionize your understanding of Lucifer and other "fallen" angels. And learn from Conway's own personal experiences, which reinforce the profound impact these spirit teachers can have on our lives.

978-0-7387-1124-9, 192 pp., 6 x 9   **$17.95**

BY THE AUTHOR OF
SPIRIT GUIDES &
ANGEL GUARDIANS

PRAYING
WITH
ANGELS

RICHARD
WEBSTER

Praying with Angels
Richard Webster

Reverence for angels spans culture, faith, and time. But can these celestial messengers answer our prayers?

Praying with Angels can help you develop a rewarding, lifelong relationship with these divine creatures. From prayer to dreamwork, you'll explore a myriad of simple ways to communicate with angels. There are practical exercises and meditations to aid in developing angel awareness—an important first step towards angelic communication. Webster also provides a fascinating tour of the angelic kingdom, revealing the role and strengths of guardian angels, angels of the zodiac, elemental angels, and others. This crucial information lays the groundwork to help you select the appropriate angel to contact according to your unique circumstances. Praying with Angels also includes rituals and techniques for requesting healing, protection, abundance, and personal guidance.

978-0-7387-1098-3, 240 pp., 5³⁄₁₆ x 8   **$20.99**

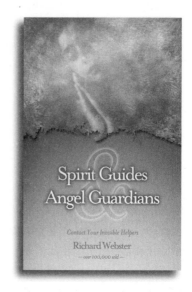

Spirit Guides
& Angel Guardians

Contact Your Invisible Helpers

Richard Webster

— over 100,000 sold —

Spirit Guides & Angel Guardians
Contact Your Invisible Helpers
RICHARD WEBSTER

They come to our aid when we least expect it, and they disappear as soon as their work is done. Invisible helpers are available to all of us; in fact, we all regularly receive messages from our guardian angels and spirit guides but usually fail to recognize them. This book will help you to realize when this occurs. And when you carry out the exercises provided, you will be able to communicate freely with both your guardian angels and spirit guides.

You will see your spiritual and personal growth take a huge leap forward as soon as you welcome your angels and guides into your life. This book contains numerous case studies that show how angels have touched the lives of others, just like yourself. Experience more fun, happiness, and fulfillment than ever before. Other people will also notice the difference as you become calmer, more relaxed, and more loving than ever before.

978-1-5671-8795-3, 368 pp., 5³⁄₁₆ x 8   **$12.95**

To order, call 1-877-NEW-WRLD
Prices subject to change without notice
Order at Llewellyn.com 24 hours a day, 7 days a week!

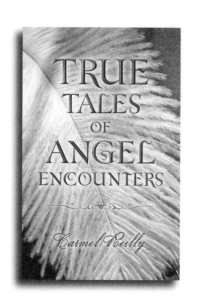

TRUE
TALES
OF
ANGEL
ENCOUNTERS

Carmel Reilly

True Tales of Angel Encounters
CARMEL REILLY

A distraught mother thinks twice about abandoning her family, a junkie is inspired to kick the habit, and a young man on the verge of insanity makes a remarkable recovery—thanks to the divine intervention of angels.

Ordinary people of diverse faiths, including the non-religious, have experienced the wonder of angels. This inspiring collection of true accounts highlights how these spiritual beings—manifesting as a kind stranger, a radiant figure, a gentle voice, or a comforting presence—have touched lives around the world. Breathtaking and heart-warming, these personal tales offer a convincing glimpse of angels at work—protecting children, offering advice during a crisis, healing babies, comforting the bereft and the dying, bringing messages from loved ones who have passed on, easing pain, and offering strength at the darkest hour.

True Tales of Angel Encounters is a glorious exploration of the human/angel relationship that's sure to reinvigorate your faith in the Divine.

978-0-7387-1494-3, 312 pp., 5³⁄₁₆ x 8 $15.95
